KU-210-916

PLANET SPORT

Sport generates some of the most intense feelings and levels of commitment. It is big business globally, but also the source of the most powerful personal identifications and individual and collective pleasures. Sporting events are routine and embodied, whether in the gym, on the field or at the training ground, and they are also spectacular, for example in mega events at the stadium or, for followers at a distance, through the media of television, radio and the Internet. Large numbers of people are caught up in personal and collective investment and public engagement with sport. Why does it matter so much?

In this book, Woodward demonstrates why sport matters and how, arguing that we should take sport seriously, and explore what is social about it. Sport is not just another domain to which social theories can be applied; it is also distinctive and generates new ways of thinking about social issues and debates. Sport is affected by the global economy and social, political and cultural processes – but it also shapes the wider social terrain of which it is part. Sport reproduces inequalities as well as offering opportunities. It is not always a level playing field. Sport is more than play.

Planet Sport is an engaging and concise introduction to some of the big issues in contemporary debates about sport in globalised societies, and will appeal to students, academics and general readers alike.

Kath Woodward is Professor of Sociology at the Open University and has published extensively on the subject of sport, including *Sex, Power and the Games* (Palgrave, forthcoming 2012), *Embodied Sporting Practices* (Palgrave, 2009), and *Boxing, Masculinity and Identity: the 'I' of the Tiger* (Routledge, 2007). Her introduction to the *Social Sciences: The Big Issues* (Routledge) is in its second edition. She is building a collection for the British Library on sex, gender and the games for the 2012 Olympics and has contributed to the Summer Games website.

SHORTCUTS – *'Little Books on Big Issues'*

Shortcuts is a major new series of concise, accessible introductions to some of the major issues of our times. The series is developed as an A to Z coverage of emergent or new social, cultural and political phenomena. Issues and topics covered range from Google to global finance, from climate change to the new capitalism, from Blogs to the future of books. Whilst the principal focus of *Shortcuts* is the relevance of current issues, topics, debates and thinkers to the social sciences and humanities, the books should also appeal to a wider audience seeking guidance on how to engage with today's leading social, political and philosophical debates.

Series Editor: Anthony Elliott is a social theorist, writer and Chair in the Department of Sociology at Flinders University, Australia. He is also Visiting Research Professor in the Departments of Sociology at the Open University, UK, and University College Dublin, Ireland. His writings have been published in sixteen languages, and he has written widely on, amongst other topics, identity, globalisation, society, celebrity and mobilities.

Titles in the series:

PLANET SPORT

Kath Woodward

Routledge
Taylor & Francis Group

LONDON AND NEW YORK

First published 2012
by Routledge
2 Park Square, Milton Park, Abingdon, Oxon,
OX14 4RN

Simultaneously published in the USA and Canada
by Routledge
711 Third Avenue, New York, NY 10017

*Routledge is an imprint of the Taylor & Francis Group,
an informa business*

© 2012 Kath Woodward

All rights reserved. No part of this book may be
reprinted or reproduced or utilised in any form or by
any electronic, mechanical, or other means, now
known or hereafter invented, including photocopying
and recording, or in any information storage or
retrieval system, without permission in writing from
the publishers.

Trademark notice: Product or corporate names may be
trademarks or registered trademarks, and are used only
for identification and explanation without intent
to infringe.

British Library Cataloguing in Publication Data
A catalogue record for this book is available from the
British Library

Library of Congress Cataloging in Publication Data
Woodward, Kath.
Planet sport / Kath Woodward.
p. cm. – (Shortcuts)
Includes bibliographical references and index.
1. Sports–Sociological aspects. 2. Sports and
globalization. 3. Sports–Cross-cultural studies. I. Title.
GV706.5.W664 2012
306.4'83–dc23   2011052535

ISBN: 978-0-415-68111-7 (hbk)
ISBN: 978-0-415-68112-4 (pbk)
ISBN: 978-0-203-80522-0 (ebk)

Typeset in Bembo
by Taylor & Francis books

BLACKBURN COLLEGE
LIBRARY

Acc. No. BB45604
Class No. 306.483 WOO
Date JUN 13

MIX
Paper from
responsible sources
FSC
www.fsc.org   FSC® C004839

Printed and bound in Great Britain by
CPI Group (UK) Ltd, Croydon, CR0 4YY

To Steve

CONTENTS

ACKNOWLEDGEMENTS

I am grateful to Anthony Elliott for his inspiration for the Shortcuts series and support for the inclusion of sport in the project and to Dr Steve Woodward for doing the index for *Planet Sport*. I am also grateful to the team at Taylor & Francis, especially Emily Briggs, and to copyeditor Liz Riley.

1

HOLD THE BACK PAGE; SPORT MATTERS

What is it about sport? Is sport just about play, albeit play that has a big role in global economies? Could sport be a set of activities reserved for the back pages of newspapers, special supplements, club websites and apps: a boys' own world of competitive aggression, pseudo heroics, memories of past glories and defeats, measurement and records? *Planet Sport* presents a strong counter argument and puts sport on the agenda as something worthy of serious academic study and intellectual engagement. The global popularity and scope of sport means you cannot ignore it. Sport brings people together in huge numbers as spectators, whether at the event or at a distance, watching on satellite television and the Internet, for example for mega events, not the least of which is the Olympic Games, billed as the greatest show on earth. Sport also secures inequalities and social divisions, however, in ways that can be assumed and taken for granted, as well as being explicitly embedded in its regulatory frameworks. Sport often presents a very unequal playing field.

Sport is not just public display; it is also personal passion and brings together the energies and intensities of social and psychic worlds in distinctive ways. Sport generates some of the most intense feelings and levels of commitment that are lived through enfleshed engagement and body practices. People really care about what happens. The quotation attributed to Bill Shankly, then manager of Liverpool Football Club, on the extremes of fan commitment to their team in the UK city of Liverpool, reflecting upon the commitment of the fans of the city's two teams, Liverpool and Everton, expresses both the hyperbole that can characterise sport, in this case of men's football, and its deep, powerful and passionate links to community:

> Some people believe football is a matter of life and death, I am very disappointed with that attitude. I can assure you it is much, much more important than that.
>
> *(Goldblatt, 2007)*

Sport provides some of the most intense identifications that can take over other aspects of daily life. When the Milwaukee Braves baseball team beat the New York Yankees of the American League, 5–0 in 1957, a whole city came to a standstill (Baseball Milwaukee, 2011). Sport includes the ambivalences and tensions between diverse elements including healthy embodied practices, excitement, passionate loyalties, excess and uncertain outcomes.

This book demonstrates why sport matters and how, by arguing that we should take sport seriously and explore what is social about sport. Sport is not just another domain to which social theories can be applied, sport is also distinctive and generates new ways of thinking about social issues and debates. Sport is affected by the global economy and social, political and cultural processes, but also has effects on the wider social terrain of which it is part. Sport is much more than play.

Sport is particular in its combination of personal pleasures and pain, embodied practices, collective commitment and globalised politics and conflicts. Sporting events are also sites of resistance and protest as well as the reiteration of traditions and conformity. Sport is divisive and collaborative, conflictual and democratic; it combines people in very particular, positive and energising ways, but also recreates tensions, ambivalences, hostilities and conflicts. The role and status of sport in contemporary societies is thus crucial to an understanding of the nature of social and cultural change as part of the iterative practices of micro narratives and encounters as well as being part of global transformations.

Sporting events are routine, whether in the gym or at the training ground, but they are also spectacular, for example in mega events at the stadium, such as the the National Football League Super Bowl in the USA or, for followers at a distance, through the media of television, radio and the Internet. The Olympics with its massive global audiences must be the mega event par excellence. Large numbers of people are caught up in personal and collective investment and public engagement with sport. The intensities of personal commitment and engagement, and sport's competitive expressivities and enfleshed actualities and its reach, scale and scope that make sport matter, are all implicated in the mix.

Planet Sport highlights some of the big issues in contemporary debates about sport in globalised societies that have been raised in sports studies and social, political and cultural commentary, to provide some explanation and arguments about how and why sport matters across the globe. It is not all about size and scope. Sport offers a route into an understanding of the pleasure and pain that operates at personal and psychic levels too. Sport lends itself particularly well to psychosocial and psychoanalytic debates about the generation of affect and of collective as well as individual processes of psychic investment and of excess as something beyond social constructivism. Sport is a social phenomenon, or set of phenomena, but sport is also outside the social in the passions it generates and to which it is subject.

The intensities that offer the promise of transcendence have been expressed as 'being in the zone', which is a phrase that has particular resonance in sport for participants and spectators and followers. Analysis of being in the zone has often focused on the internal states of individuals, deriving from psychology (Csikzentimihalyi, 1995), which may have underestimated the importance of culture to heightened creative performance and the cultural significance of achieving a personal best. In sport the two combine most strikingly. The internal emotions of athletes, like those of musicians or creative workers, suggest experience of heightened competence, but also the cultural framework in which the very distinction between 'routine' and 'peak' is created; the distinguishing dimensions of sport are its everyday practices and its sensational spectacles.

Being in the zone has been applied to such experiences that go beyond the discursive in engagement in practices such as sport and artistic fields. Participants experience either transcendence from routine practice that is difficult to classify and express, or a harmony and synchrony that in sport is always in some way primarily enfleshed and sentient. Being in the zone is rarely a conscious expression of experience of the moment but it is one that elevates sport beyond 'mere play' and links sport most strongly to other cultural practices.

In Alan Sillitoe's (2007) short story, *The Loneliness of the Long Distance Runner*, and even more centrally in the film of the same name, the central character, an inmate of a borstal (as youth offender detention centres were then called), participates in a running competition. Sillitoe's description of the experience, expressed as a first-person internal narrative, demonstrates well the phenomenon of the zone and the possible conflicts and contradictions between the harmony and synchrony of elevated embodied experience and resistance to the competitive imperative of rule-governed sport. His first-person account is of a feeling 'so smooth I forgot I was running'. However, in spite of the borstal governor's encouragement and entreaties that he could become a professional athlete when he leaves the prison, the young man stops before the finishing line in the final race between institutions for the Borstal Blue Ribbon prize. Being in the zone in sport does not necessarily mean conforming to the rules of competition; rules can be broken and the activity remain sport.

Sport challenges the binary split of mind and body. The zone is also used to describe some of the fluid movements of sport where everything is right and mind and body are synchronised, for example, as in cricket when bowlers 'get their eye in' without having to think about the specificities of the corporeal action, or a boxer keeps going in spite of extensive injury that the boxer appears not to feel. This is not only about individual athletic performance or elite performance; the zone can be a democratic, collective space that brings people together. Sport affords not only the promise of individual transcendent experiences, but also the possibility that such moments can be shared through collective engagement and through cultural representations.

Sport inspires diverse artistic and cultural representations that transgress the boundaries between high and low or popular cultures, notably in writing but also in art and sculpture (Woodward, 2011, 2012) and in film where, for example, boxing has generated some of the most highly acclaimed films such as Martin Scorsese's *Raging Bull*. In the US, the writing of Mark Twain, Norman Mailer, Joyce Carol Oates's (1987) *On Boxing*, Daniel O'Connor's collection on Mike Tyson, Lionel Shriver on snooker, George Plimpton, Damon Runyon, Robert Coover's (1971) *The Universal Baseball Association* or Don de Lillo's coverage of baseball at the start of *Tokyo Underworld* (Whiting, 1971), are just a few examples. Men's football has generated examples in the UK, such as Nick Hornby's (2010) *Fever Pitch* and Simon Kuper's (2003) *Football Against the Enemy*, but the field is more restricted.

Sports historians have produced some really great work that, for example in cricket writing, has had considerable impact;

C. L. R. James, Mike Marqusee and Ashis Nandy have each embraced the politics of sport and demonstrated the intensities of cricket as a mode of expression. There are sports histories that present a narrative of particular sports but sport is often absent in historical accounts, even those that engage with journalism and broadcast media. Briggs' epic five volume account of the BBC (1995) has no specific sections on sport, although clearly sport was central to the making of Britishness as it was developed in the BBC's mission and vision of impartiality and fair play, set down by Lord Reith (Scannell and Cardiff, 1991). Sport is mentioned of course, for example in the development of outside broadcasting as part of the seamless cycle of the season in British life, but not addressed as a distinctive, separate part of the service worthy of discussion in its own right (Woodward, 2009) even though it permeates Briggs' narrative. The annual BBC Reith Lectures have never focused specifically on sport. There is nervousness about crossing the boundary between the serious streams of art, literature and history and the playful narratives of sport. Sport remains a source of the most powerful personal identifications and individual and collective pleasures and pain, although as a field of study it may be trivialised because of its strong associations with play.

Sport is a central part of contemporary life and widely enmeshed with and constitutive of social relations and social divisions; planet sport is made up of the intersection of very different power axes. For example, whilst in the wider cultural and social terrain of western neoliberal democracies categories of sex gender may be seen as more fluid, in sport the binary logic of sex persists, albeit largely called gender in the contemporary discourse of sport. The vast majority of sports are classified as women's or men's competitions, even though men's are not always marked, as in the football 'World Cup'; the female counterpart of which is the 'Women's World Cup'. The ways in which networks of hegemonic masculinity endure make sport a rich field for research into social and cultural continuities as well as change, especially as more women worldwide are joining in and enjoying the pleasures of sport as well as its rigorous regimes.

The technologies of enhancement through training, nutrition and less legal and legitimate pharmaceutical interventions may be fast moving and transformative but the field of sport manifests significant endurances, especially in the inequalities of some of its practices and mechanisms. Attempts in sport, for example by the International Olympics Committee (IOC) and International Association of Athletics Federations (IAAF), to establish some kind of certainty about categories of sex gender through 'gender verification' are instructive about the making and shaping of gender in contemporary societies. Sport is social and there are good reasons why sport often makes the front pages as well as the back pages and sports supplements. This book offers some explanations of how and why, starting with the classificatory systems that understandings of sport draw upon and what might be included under the heading of sport.

2

WHAT COUNTS AS SPORT

How and why?

Whatever else it is, sport is in some part organised play. Sport's ludic dimensions, facilitating playful experiences and germinating excitement have been central to many accounts by those who have mapped out the field in sports studies (such as Guttmann, 2005; Giulianotti, 2005; Ingham and Loy, 1993; Loy, 1968; McPherson *et al.*, 1989). Play, increased leisure time and extended periods of childhood are all part of the modern and post-modern condition, which are aligned with the huge expansion of sport in the twentieth and twenty-first centuries. Sport has players who step out of their conventional roles and perform new ones on a stage that is both entertaining and challenging in a variety of ways, although it is also increasingly work, of course, for many of those who engage in its practices both on and off the field.

Sport in its classification both illustrates and challenges the dualistic thinking that separates the instrumentally rational from the affective and value-driven, as illustrated by Ferdinand Tönnies' distinction between Gemienschaft and Gescelleschaft

(1957) and in Max Weber's theory of rationalisation (2003 [1905]). There are elements of exuberance in what counts as sport in the feelings of well being and exhilaration of physical exertion and the pleasure and freedom of movement. Sport has the capacity to generate these feelings as Mary Wollstonecraft recognised in her *Vindication of the Rights of Woman* first published in 1792, where she argued that women would never gain independence while little girls were physically constrained and did not enjoy the free embodied movement with which their brothers could engage. There is an exuberance and joy in sporting activity that makes it more than a trivial activity. Wollstonecraft argued that women need strength of mind and body and the freedom that accompanies physical activity. She recommended that mothers permit their daughters as well as their sons the opportunity to engage in some of the pleasures of sport and 'frolic in the open air'. The pleasures of such embodied activities and the freedom of expression they promise challenge some of the rigidity of definitions of sport that stress the primacy of regulatory measures and rule-governed practice. Some of these challenges are present in contemporary, alternative, extreme or postmodern sports in which people who are marginalised by the traditional organising bodies of sport engage (Rinehart and Sydnor, 2003, 2010).

We do sport, whether as practitioners, supporters or followers, mostly because we want to and it is pleasurable. Sport is also increasingly instrumental for individuals however, for example through the body projects that characterise contemporary societies (Shilling, 2008). Contemporary western liberal imperatives to utilise body projects in the regulatory practices of technologies of the self are often located within the field of sport because of sport's merging of body and self and its embodied disciplinary regimes.

What have been called body projects offer both an example of the widening of the categories of sport, because they involve bodily practices, disciplinary, regulated regimens and elements of pleasure and well being, and the ways in which sport is crossing into other areas of social and cultural life. Body projects are also intensely individualistic programmes of self improvement and of what Nikolas Rose (1996) called psy discourses, albeit more corporeal than other aspects of the integration of the psychic with the social in contemporary life. The body project, working out in the gym, or at home, in different social spaces, with a personal trainer, often with extreme degrees of personal commitment, sometimes linked to reworking the self through the flesh through cosmetic surgery of therapeutic interventions, crosses the boundaries of what can be called sport, but nonetheless has elements of a reconfigured notion of sport. It is also competitive if not in the conventional language of competing teams.

Sport is also instrumental in that it generates income for many who are involved in the social worlds of sport, for communities and even for nations and the states that govern them. However, a component of what is classified as sport always has aspects of its pleasurable sides. Sport is not just play, although the joy of frolicking in the fresh air and elevated pleasurable experiences are part of it, because it also carries disciplinary, regulatory dimensions. Sporting success can only be achieved through practice and routine engagement, but nonetheless sport can generate its own intense feelings, emotions and expressions.

Whatever its links to play, sport also has its own if somewhat contradictory rationales. It may necessarily involve pleasure, but it is also about winning; as the legendary US football coach of the 1950s, Vince Lombardi reputedly said 'Winning is not a sometime thing; it's an all time thing'. Winning and losing are also based on measurement. Modern sport always demands technologies of quantification and record keeping. Distances, speeds, times have to be measured through increasingly high-specification technologies in order to gauge success and attribute achievement.

Clearly sport is not only about winning; most people, most teams lose most of the time, but there are ambiguities in a set of activities that is supposedly play, being mainly concerned with success and winning. It is also possible to be in the zone without winning. Winning also deals in aspirations, desires and the fulfilment of dreams. Winning may be the goal that most of us never achieve, but it is always a psychic possibility; a promise of what might be, even if only in our dreams and fantasies, and this too is part of what makes sport. Promises of success and heroic narratives and practices like scoring the 'glory goal' are in a sense a component if not always directly acknowledged in the sports studies literature of sport.

The promise of sporting heroics occupies inner worlds that may be shaped by the social worlds in which such narratives of heroism are written, but they are not always consonant and sport offers pleasures that may defy regulation and challenge the disciplinary regimes, as the example of *The Loneliness of the Long Distance Runner* demonstrates so well. Even if they are broken there still have to be rules to break.

Much of the literature on classifying and defining sport stresses the description of this form of play as organised. Guttmann (2005) argues that modern sport has transformed from its pre-modern more playful forms into highly organised sets of engagement, which are themselves now challenged by what has been called postmodern sport in democratised forms, whereby practitioners seek to write their own rules, as in for example parkour with its apparently free flowing techniques of negotiating movement around objects in urban spaces. Parkour is free running but it is already generating its own regulatory frameworks and shared techniques. It remains, however, avowedly non competitive and its rules are not imposed from above by non practitioners. There are still rules of course, but the rules belong to those who act and do, rather than formalised regulatory bodies responsible for the surveillance and monitoring of sport. Organised play cannot be entirely spontaneous; there has largely been some agreement about what constitutes the rules. In most cases, these rules have to be made and constantly recreated and refined by the organising bodies of what traditionally counts as sport. Some of these bodies have huge global reach, such as the IOC, which has 204 member states with National Olympic Committees (NOCs) across five continents. Organisation thus operates at a global level and crosses the boundaries of nation states and local practices.

Sports sociologists have stressed the centrality of the rule-governed nature of sport combined with its regulatory frameworks; sport is fun but it is also rule governed. The twentieth and twenty-first centuries have seen an explosion of rules and rule changes. A regulatory framework is also important, not only because we all need to be playing to the same set of rules, but also because sport largely involves contests and competition and there needs to be an acceptance of a level playing field and a sense of fairness and justice in both the practices of play and the adjudication of outcomes. There are challenges to the highly competitive nature of contemporary sport, many of which also suggest the possibilities of endeavouring to achieve a personal best; you are still competing if only against yourself.

Allen Guttmann emphasises how the 'rules of the game' are crucial to the interrelationship between play, games and contests, which is what, he argues, makes modern sport (Guttmann, 2005). The spontaneous, autotelic play of pre-modern societies is transformed into games through the application of rules, which themselves demand regulatory bodies to create and then monitor and police those rules; a point at which politics becomes formally involved with sport.

Guttmann's definitions are also underpinned by a separation of mind and body and of the intellectual and corporeal in what also differentiates between sports that require physical prowess, such as football, and those that do not, a category that he illustrates by Scrabble and chess, as activities that require more intellectual investment than, for example, sprinting. He acknowledges the problems inherent in the mind, body and flesh intellect, binaries, because admittedly the boundaries of categorisation are leaky.

Some sports may not immediately appear to be physically demanding and in many sports there is no contact between the bodies of those who participate. Some sports may be also less obviously demanding of elite physical fitness than others. The associations of darts with inactivity, what might appear to be a lack of the fit, honed, slender body, and drinking beer might call into question its status as a sport, but it demands concentration and it is highly competitive. The embodied practices of darts are classified as sport by the regulatory apparatuses that thus entail its inclusion in the category of sport. Motor racing, such as Formula One and Indianapolis 500, are sports where there is not body contact or even much physical movement, or only that which is mechanically propelled. Sports such as car racing demand endurance, mental agility and elite physical fitness, and competition and conflict can be just as intense and conflictual without bodies coming into direct contact. Car racing is also highly competitive, as well as being dangerous with events such as the Indy at times having more in common with Russian roulette than team games or even boxing where at least the dangers are obvious. There are moments when risk materialises into unacceptable danger, as for example in the fifteen-car Indy crash in Las Vegas in 2011 when Dan Wheldon lost his life. He took risks for a living, but there are elements in the organisation and regulation of sport where the level of risk is too high and has to be regulated too. This negotiation between acceptable and unacceptable risk is one that characterises sport.

The element of risk and uncertainty about outcomes is a feature of some sports more than others, but some trace of insecurity and uncertainty, if not explicitly danger, is always present. Danger and uncertainty are part of what makes sport and is constitutive of its attractions. Outcomes are not predictable, which is also why sport and gambling are so attracted to each other. At some points in the history of sport the two have been synonymous; gambling is sport.

The centrality of bodies, body practices and flesh in sport, highlight these issues.

Bodies, embodied practices and enfleshed selves dominate the field of sport and its pleasures, pains and competences and its classificatory systems. Boxers are classified by weight and body mass is crucial in matching opponents; to fight out of your weight could pose considerable risks. Most notably, corporeal characteristics are used to determine who can and who cannot participate in which sports. For example, having a body classified as female has kept women out of a large number of sports: boxing for most of the twentieth century, marathon and long-distance running and sprinting to name but a few. Other sports such as golf and polo give more weight to the intersection of sex gender with the specificities of class, race and ethnicity. Women's and men's competitions are separate in all but a very few sports (mixed doubles in tennis, mixed foursomes in golf, but sex is still the determinant). Sports have different rules for women and men competitors; shorter tees in golf, shorter distances in track and field and fewer rounds in boxing. Measurement and classification, which are constitutive of en-fleshed participants too, are central to sporting regimes of truth.

The classification of people into racial categories has played a key role in segregation in sport by means of criteria of visible corporeal difference too. Race and racialisation have been ele-ments in the classificatory systems of sport and are constitutive of racialised categories in other social worlds. Racialisation has been a powerful element used to justify exclusion from particular sports historically by formal means and more recently still by biologically determinist essentialist discourses about racial types as well as through social and cultural forces. There has been movement from the exclusion of racialised regimes such as apartheid in South Africa and other white supremacist systems to the promotion of black athletes and even their preponderance in some events. The inclusion of black athletes in some sports and their particular success, for example of African Caribbean and African men's sprinting and long-distance running, is not all liberatory, however. The investment of physical capital (Bourdieu, 1986) can be construed as the only strategy possible for example in a sport such as boxing (WacQuant, 2004) rather than the only strategy that is formally available. Racialised, ethnicised and gendered exclusion are not so much part of the definition of sport, but what has made sport and what sport makes in the wider society. Sport has the capacities. Racialised segregation has been an explicit component of the classification of sport; some sports have enduring white associations reproduced through exclusionary practices. Struggles against racism have led to the elimination of such formalised practices of segregation, but there remain elements of racialised classification in sport, sometimes situated within discourses of scientific racism. Black athleticism can be used to support theories of racialised difference and the suitability of black people, usually men, not only for particular sports, generally not those with the distinction of association with the upper classes, such as polo and golf, but also for athletic rather than intellectual activity.

Sport classifies bodies and creates desirable bodies, beautiful bodies and of course broken, damaged bodies. In some sports, body size, especially weight is the criterion by which participation is decided, as in the weights in boxing. The body size of jockeys matters, as it does in determining which position a player takes up in rugby (prop forwards need more body mass than fly halves), and height influences positions in sports such as basketball and netball. Body size may determine positions on the field, but it is often the sexed body that shapes decisions about whether the sport is transmitted by satellite to millions across the globe, recruiting massive interest and financial investment and sponsorship. Sex gender is both an element in how sport is formally classified internally and empirically and also reproduces regimes of gender inequality outside sport. In the hierarchies of sport, body size and weight may not be innocent factors. Basketball occupies a more privileged position in the taxonomies of sport than netball, and baseball than rounders, because of the sexed bodies of the participants that are enmeshed in the power geometries of sport and the wider social terrain.

This does, however, raise questions about why some activities count as sport and is there a hierarchy of sports? There is limited acceptance although there is some acknowledgement that it is men who have written the rules and thus, as Guttmann mentions, domestic activities undertaken by women, such as weaving, horticulture and corn husking have not been classified as sports whereas the log-rolling and ploughing associated with men have. This is clearly not only a matter of physical strength. Neither is it, as Guttmann suggests, only a matter of women's sporting competitions having been hidden from history, although as feminist sports historians have shown, this is an important dimension of inequality (Hargreaves *et al.*, 2007; Hargreaves, 1994, 2000).

The making of sporting rules has also been racialised in the intersections between sport and politics. There are strands in the genealogies of sport in which forces of inequality and social divisions such as those of social class, gender, ethnicity and race intersect. Sport has a long history of racialised segregation that challenged any suggestions that the definitions of sport and its classificatory systems are not politically informed. Politics has dominated sport in places as diverse as Nazi Germany, the USA during the period of racial segregation and South Africa in the apartheid era when boycotts became the most powerful tool of resistance. Racism in sport has most strongly militated against competitions between people classified as belonging to particular racial or ethnic groups; fights between black and white boxers were banned in the US for a long period of time (Simmons, 1988). At some periods in sporting history the politics of inequality played out through institutionalised exclusions, at others through less formal mechanisms, such the impossibility of black players joining the clubs of the sports of the affluent, privileged white classes, such as golf clubs. Class and racialisation are widely imbricated in the politics of sport. Recognition of the processes of exclusion has been one step along the way to promoting diversity, albeit a very slow step in many sports.

Regulatory bodies make sport and classify which ones count. For 2012 'new' sports such as women's boxing were included in the Olympics, which nonetheless raises questions about how such decisions are made and what are the points of connection between different systems and processes in how sport is classified and defined. The IOC is informed by other organisations and has responsibility for making the final decisions. Some sports have mass spectatorship and high status, such as basketball, whereas a sport that involves similar rules and practices, such as netball, does not. The existing regulatory bodies of sport are faced with problems of accommodating the alternative or extreme sports that challenge existing competitive practices and governance that have traditionally been what makes modern sport.

The explosion of rules by sports regulatory bodies might conceal the obverse, which is rule breaking. It is both the element of chance and the possibility of at least bending the rules that also makes sport. Sport involves setting standards of achievement and of winning and losing, albeit in a context of some uncertainty. It is hardly surprising that sport has a long history of associations with betting and one of the attempts to secure certainty of outcomes is match fixing. Consequently, another massive problem for the regulatory bodies of sport is that of corruption. Sport has also been beset by accusations of corruption that resonate far beyond the fields of sport itself. Corrupt practices relate to match fixing, drug taking and the influence of gambling on sport; in the case of gambling, this is somewhat ironic since both the origins of sport and its very raison d'être is that it is a game of chance. Modern sport is closely implicated with field sports involving betting on the outcomes: horse racing, prize fighting, cock fighting and dog fighting and all the gaming activities of the Fancy described by Pierce Egan in the early nineteenth century (Egan, 2006 [1812]). Sporting competitions are all about uncertain outcomes; the problems arise when there is interference in the outcome prior to the competition for personal gain. Global sport in the twenty-first century is subject to a massive range of possible interventions to enhance performance, the speed of flows of information made possible by the web and complex networks that are able to avoid detection. Also the temptations of succumbing to corrupt practices are great in financial terms. Some accusations of corruption have been made against the regulatory bodies of sport themselves: the IOC in the bidding process for Salt Lake City and more recently at the Fédération Internationale de Football Association (FIFA), the governing body of world football.

These examples raise questions about how sport is defined and are used to explain some of the different dimensions of sport, its structures, rules, regulations and practices as well as, most importantly, the processes through which sport is enmeshed in social, political and cultural relations. Sport, however, has been repeatedly and avowedly disassociated from politics with publicly voiced platitudes, admittedly more from politicians and sports journalists than academics of sport, averring that sport and politics do not mix or that politics must not be allowed to contaminate sport. Sport sociologists have demonstrated the absurdity of these claims, but nonetheless there is some anxiety about the relationship between sport and politics, the traces of which persist in popular cultural expressions such as the disavowal of the political aspects of what is sport, the claims that sport and politics do not mix or keep politics out of sport. Not only is sport inherently political, it is also implicated in and constitutive of politics at all levels, from the personal that is political to the structural and the global.

One of the most obvious manifestations of planet sport is the global reach of those activities that are classified under the heading of sport. Sport is played, watched, followed, discussed and closely implicated with aspects of the economy and social and cultural life everywhere in the world. The specificities of global and local sport are particular to their locations. Who plays which sport and where are dimensions of sport's global scope, which generate important political questions. Its global reach is all part of what makes up modern sport and lends weight to claims about sport's universal capacities and properties.

Globalisation is not such a new phenomenon in sport as some globalisers might have claimed for the world political economy. Sport is global; all societies have some form of sporting engagement and sport travels in that there are many more supporters of UK Premiership clubs such as Manchester United in China than there are in the UK. However, the map of global sport demonstrates the specificities of planet sport. Some sports do not traverse national boundaries in the way others do and different parts of the world have different sporting traditions. Sport is also closely tied up with empire and with colonialism. Global reach and globalisation are key elements in the make-up of planet sport and in thinking about its impact upon social and political relations, forces, flows and networks. The global dimensions of sport are part of the definition of sport in the contemporary world, as are the points of connections between the global and the local and the ways in which these can be routinely played out in the g/local.

3

THIS SPORTING PLANET

G/local sport

Global forces weave their way through sport creating new synergies and affiliations making and remaking transnational flows. There is the flow of capital investment and the allied activities, especially those relating to sponsorship and media and broadcast networks as well as the transfer of players and of the cultural products of sport that create new alliances and configurations of identification. The global reach and ubiquity of satellite coverage and transmission of sporting events make new affiliations possible and inevitable; evidenced in the branding that is made visible in the strip of English Premiership clubs such as Manchester United that dominates unexpected locations such as the spectator stands at the African Cup of Nations.

Sport, however defined, is global in that there are sporting activities in all parts of the world and increasingly sport crosses the boundaries of nations. Sport is regulated and managed by transnational bodies and elite athletes are highly mobile, in more ways than one, as are the sponsorship flows that promote and support them. Sport has in some ways been ahead of global economics and political economy in recognising, reconfiguring and engaging with the concept of the nation state, the limitations of which have become all too apparent in the global economic crises that began in the summer of 2007 and erupted with the collapse of Lehman Brothers and the subsequent global banking crisis in 2008 followed by the Eurozone crisis of 2011. The issue of the precedence often taken by clubs over national teams and the identification with a league or club across the boundaries of nation or even continent have been debated in sport for some time.

'World' is a word that features in the language of sport. International competitions are the mega events that pull the punters; the Olympics and competitions such as the men's football World Cup attract massive viewing figures: 1 billion, 15 per cent of the world population watched the Beijing Olympics opening ceremony and FIFA estimated 715 million for the 2010 South Africa men's World Cup final. In the golden age of boxing a heavyweight fight such as the 1971 'Fight of the Century' between Joe Frazier and Muhammad Ali is reported to have attracted audiences of 300 million worldwide. Boxing is a more individualised sport with less emphasis on national allegiance and more on cultural and ethnic belongings, but it incorporates nation and national identifications in different ways. Nation states and identification with the nation are important in different ways; national sides with traditional expertise and affiliations compete in the major international tournaments and individuals represent their countries in athletics and the Olympics. Such competitions bring together diverse nations, reinstating as well as crossing national boundaries; nation states matter in particular ways and in particular places in sport. The nation plays a more visible part in the Olympics than in many other mega events, for example in the opening ceremonies.

A stress on the international and transnational elements of sport can underplay the powerful expressions of emotion and collective commitment that accompany pivotal points, particular competitions in some sports when people come together to identify with the nation in what is more than an imagined community: an expressive, emotive community. As a life-long fan of Welsh rugby, I have personal investment in the moments at Cardiff Arms Park, now transferred to the Millennium Stadium, when the intensity of collective emotion, often expressed in song, was equally strong whatever the outcome, but nothing can compare with defeating England and the incomprehensible pride in the nation, however small the nation and however long its time more or less under English rule.

Such feelings can also be associated with a club or a team, of course especially in old firm derbies, for example the two clubs in a city, such as Everton and Liverpool, or more powerfully between the Glasgow football teams Celtic and Rangers, where the strength of emotions have long and complex genealogies that are a complicated mix of religious, political, cultural and national elements, as well as very contemporary expressions and manifestations.

National identifications can be transnational too of course and most fans have a ranking order of nations either that they hope to defeat or that they would want to win if their own team is unsuccessful.

Sports are regulated and governed by transnational and international bodies and the people who play for the top clubs and teams in many sports are less likely to be local. The global distributions of modern and postmodern sport, post imperialism, range from the legacies of empire to the democratising possibilities of sport. The global distribution of sport has in many cases been seen to be in conversation with or as a reaction to empire, for example in the case of cricket that has travelled from the game of empire to the Indian Premier League (IPL), and some sports have taken off in different ways in different places, for example in the US, Japan and Australia. Looking at the global also provides a route into evaluating how the flows and forces of globalisation play out in different ways in sport as well as the democratic possibilities of global sport within mainstream and alternative sport.

Looking at the global also involves paying some attention to globalisation and the dimensions of the processes that have rendered globalisation such a familiar explanatory tool over the last thirty years or so and a genuine buzz word for our era (Lemert *et al.*, 2010). In sport, the second half of the twentieth century following the Second World War saw a version of globalisation in which sport was widely imbricated. Sport increasingly became part of the processes of wider cultural, political and economic transformations that have accelerated in the wake of high-speed communication networks and knowledge flows. The interconnected impact of television, commercialisation and sponsorship has transformed the sporting landscape and provided interconnections between sport and cultural diplomacy as well as highlighting international tensions and conflicts.

Planet sport invokes both global reach and the extension of sports and sporting practices across the globe, and the universal interest and excitement that sport can be seen to inspire; sport is played everywhere and it is a large-scale, cultural, social and financial concern. Some aspects of the explosion of interest in the concept and phenomenon of globalisation from the latter part of the twentieth century are particularly well represented in sport, through synergies notably between the speed of communication flows and information networks and the investment of global capital in organisations such as Rupert Murdoch's media empire that funds them.

The processes of globalisation embrace the complex intersection of economic, social, cultural and political factors through both points of connection and absorption and points of disruption and disconnection.

The ubiquity of theories of globalisation might have led to their utility being questioned to the extent that they might seem almost redundant as a means of explaining social relations and transformations and relegated to taken-for-granted description.

Sport like other cultural phenomena has strongly localised aspects. The emphasis on processes and mobilities in theories of globalisation, however, means that they have a great deal to offer. Globalism in sport and the globalisation of sport are distinctive as well as reflective of the massive interest there has been in the phenomenon and the debate about what constitutes globalisation in the contemporary world.

Globalisation has been characterised by the crossing of borders and the reconfiguration and even elimination of boundaries that distinguish internationalisation. Cross-border exchanges dominate global sport with the trade in players and the increased number of international competition circuits. The breakdown of boundaries, not only between nations and continents but also between different groups of people, has contributed to arguments about the 'global village' and the emergence of a growing sense of connection and a global collectivity that is visually expressed in the image of the globe seen from space as an electronic football. There may be moments when this imaginary has purchase and there can be a sense of belonging, for example at the summer Olympics, or the men's football World Cup, or a more localised mega event such as the Super Bowl. Romanticised notions of community can, however, be disrupted by the inequities that still pervade sport. The Olympics host city accommodates athletes in the Olympic Village – nomenclature that invokes a localised, traditional sense of community and resonates with the connections of the global village.

The regulatory bodies of sport, as in other fields of governance, increasingly demonstrate a liberalisation of national restrictions and the establishment of cross-border organisations such as the World Trade Organisation (WTO), the North American Free Trade Area (NAFTA) and the European Union (EU). Sport has its own international governance, such as the IOC, but cross-border organisations such as the EU have impact in sport too, as in the case of the ruling governing the transfer of players and the number of non national players that a team can field in football (the Bosman ruling). Even more significant is the liberalisation of cross-border television and broadcast media ownership.

Globalisation has also largely been recognised as universal or at least a set of powerful phenomena that have had impact everywhere in some shape or form, not least the cultural syntheses it has generated. One example is the global engagement in the Olympics through the participating countries (more than there are members of the United Nations) and especially the number of countries that receive television and, increasingly, Internet transmissions. This may seem to make for an ever more homogeneous diet of sport, although there remains enormous diversity and the routes travelled by sport and its broadcasting across the globe are far from linear, even and uniform.

Sport is embodied in ways that make its practices distinctive and diverse, even when playing by the rules, however rigidly they are applied. There were massive differences in the fluid ensemble work of the Spanish men's football team in 2010 and the tedious long-ball format of other less-successful teams. Sports are played in different ways in different places, including the adaptation of the rules, such as Australian rules football. Small-scale topographical specificities as well as particular places having distinctive games that are not played elsewhere, such as the Highland Games that celebrate Celtic heritage in Scotland, which is also home to shinty, a team game played with sticks, which it is suggested might be the precursor to ice hockey.

Although globalisation has at times been associated with Americanisation or westernisation and the transmission of western values of unregulated markets, individualism and neoliberalism, this has not always been uniformly evident in sport. In fact US sport has not travelled quite as extensively as other aspects of US culture, such as Coca-Cola or McDonald's.

What might be called rational bureaucratisation allied to technological, medical and scientific developments have permeated sport, however, wherever it is played so that sport is indeed heavily commercialised and the competitive field features a high degree of specialisation and intervention in the form of expert knowledge such as that of physiotherapists, sports psychologists and dieticians. Pharmaceutical enhancement of performance has also spread across the field of sport, although this requires a resource base that is not available to athletes in less-affluent countries, especially for those drugs that are most difficult to detect. Economic factors remain central to the mobilities and flows of globalisation, whatever position you take on its politics, although culture and economics are so widely enmeshed that it is difficult to disentangle these as separate forces.

The mobilities of globalised sport, in all its dimensions also involve de-territorialisation, whereby the spatial organisation of social relations is transformed by shifting perceptions of distance and space. The oft-mentioned fan base of Premiership clubs such as Manchester United and Manchester City, having far more fans in China or Africa than they have or have ever had in their 'home' city, is testimony to the speed of transmission of sports events as well as the massive promotion of competitions especially in a sport like men's football. More fans at the African Cup of Nations competition sport the strip of English (and Scottish in the case of Celtic and Rovers) football stars than any of those in the team of their own nation, partly because of the technologies that permit such high-quality regular broadcasts of these teams. This example also demonstrates the movement of players, especially from African countries that are the regular recruiting ground of Premiership clubs. The hopes and dreams of boys and young men are fuelled by such possibilities, so much so that there is also massive exploitation by ruthless entrepreneurs who seek to profit from this market and have no links to big clubs. The dreams and desires are personal and local and generated by the passion that sport makes possible, but that are then appropriated in the global flows for exploitative purposes. Sport occupies a space where tensions are played out in diverse ways;

the converse of the dreams of legitimate reward and publicly recognised success are the possibilities for corruption and exploitation within these global markets.

Global sport offers opportunities and its discourses are often framed by democratic ideals, as in the case of the Olympics for example, but progress towards these idealised outcomes and futures is far from linear and often marked by inequalities, which sport also facilitates through the intensities of its identifications and the aspirations that globalised sport makes thinkable. It is a complex picture and sport does not always fit neatly into the theoretical frameworks offered by conceptualisations of globalisation. Also, what actually constitutes world sport can be unexpected and not follow the routes of globalisation.

There are strong connections between particular places and particular sports, even if some sports do seem to be global in their reach. It depends what mega sporting event is taking place at the time, but even a brief look at broadcast schedules of sport indicates that the big men's team games make up a substantial part of the world's sports, for example, football, rugby union and league, and cricket, in terms of media coverage. During the Olympics sports such as rugby and cricket have a lower profile because this is a point at which track and field dominate the broadcast schedules. The biggest sports are those that dominate global broadcast media, which is illustrated by the BBC World Service coverage of the African continent where the big sports are football, athletics and boxing, although boxing no longer has quite the purchase it once had in its golden age.

In terms of how many people take part in how many places, athletics is in the lead, closely followed by men's football, which receives more media coverage than athletics, except at peak times such as international athletics championship competitions or, most dramatically, the Olympics. There are more connections between men's football and other elements of popular, celebrity culture globally, although baseball, basketball and American football certainly generate mega stars who infiltrate other domains of politics as well as popular culture and thus receive extensive media coverage.

The category 'world sports' is heavily dominated by the legacies of location, the relevance of which relates strongly to political movements and the operation of political power. The data on world sport provide viewing figures, attendance at events and sponsorship information but they are rarely broken down by gender. If amateur and participatory sports were included it is likely that jogging, yoga and swimming would exceed American football or Australian rules. In North America, American football, baseball, basketball and ice hockey matter most. American football recruits huge audiences, as does Formula One, for example the Brazilian Grand Prix. The French play football and rugby union but not rugby league or cricket; cycling is a major French sport. Australian rules football is mostly played in Australia where its embodied practices as a contact sport have strong cultural continuities. Tennis is played in many parts of the world but Wimbledon is the only major tournament played on grass.

Some sports are clearly determined by geographical locations, especially winter sports, although the motors of global capital and possibilities for profit mean that, for example, lucrative sports such as golf are increasingly finding a home in what would appear to be most inappropriate, desert terrains in the Middle East. Such developments are not surprising since hitherto it has been the G8 countries (USA, UK, France, Germany, Canada, Italy, Russia and Japan) that have dominated world sport and won most medals at the Olympics; add China and the dominance is even more complete. New markets, global recession and the Eurozone crisis mean that the fluidities of globalisation will open up new opportunities in sport too. There are strands of sporting success in particular sports, such as rugby and cricket in which Australia and New Zealand, and in the case of cricket, the Caribbean, with the great West Indies teams, have been prominent and these are parts of the world where sport routinely matters in everyday life, but there have been strong connections between economic systems and financial processes that make the economic axis of power one that has considerable influence in any argument about global sport.

Not all the world sports are team games but broadcast schedules and rights, sponsorship and commercial interest suggest a heavy emphasis on men's team sports.

An interrogation of political genealogies can provide persuasive explanation of some of the specificities of sport and the location of particular world sports. Sport has also been strongly linked to national and nationalist politics; German gymnastics and handball earlier in the twentieth century were positioned within a discourse in which healthy bodies were racialised and politicised.

The codification of sports has been traditional, for example modern winter sports were first regulated in Alpine and Nordic nations and in North America, and martial arts have strong links to Japan and Thailand. Britain was the key nation in the nineteenth century in creating both embodied practices and regulatory frameworks for many modern sports, including football, cricket, rugby, athletics and tennis, and some of the developments in these sports can be seen as in dialogue with colonialism and post colonialism. Cricket is a sport that has a particular role in this context.

From the game of empire to the IPL

Cricket, as Ashis Nandy (1989) famously said, is an Indian game accidentally discovered by the British. Cricket is a global game in that it has a significant presence on every continent except America. It has a global governing body, since 2005 based in Dubai. However, cricket, unlike football, is concentrated in Australasia, South Asia, the Caribbean and South Africa. Cricket offers an excellent example of the complex interweaving of power and non epochal change through resistance to colonialism and racism that is possible within sport.

Cricket prospered outside Britain in the twentieth century but only in the former colonies of the British empire through modes of diffusion through the agencies of empire-settler populations, the civil service, the military, the church and educational institutions as well as the BBC World Service, which routinely broadcast county cricket over test series matches if England were not playing (Woodward *et al.*, 2011). The presence of a large colonial bureaucracy and white British presence in some parts of Africa under British rule, for example in Kenya, Zimbabwe and South Africa seems to have created cricketing nations. Cricket would appear to be or at least to have been the game of empire, although not all former colonies took up the sport with any enthusiasm, such as Canada or indeed the USA.

Nandy argues, however, that despite its English roots, reflecting traditional class-based, racialised hierarchies and its divisions between 'gentlemen' and 'players', cricket also permitted a critique of the managerial, teleological values of early industrialism by asserting courtesy and respect for other players and the possibilities of playing for playing's sake along with adherence to uncodified, unstated conventions that made the sport attractive to India's elites. Much of this has been lost, however. The practice of walking (that is returning to the pavilion) if you suspect the bat touched the ball before a catch and you would be given out, whether or not this was detected by the umpire, has all but disappeared. 'New cricket' is now more closely identified with the 'industrial management ethos and so endorses the ruling culture of the contemporary world' (Nandy, 1989).

Cricket not only has cultural synergies that lend it to challenges to imperialism, it also has embodied practices that create possibilities of resistance and reconfiguration of political power relations, as C. L. R. James, the Trinidadian cricket enthusiast, writer and critic demonstrated in *Beyond a Boundary* (1963). James was the editor of the political paper, the *Nation*, the political organ of the People's National Movement when public outcry about the case for West Indian self government erupted, along with what he describes as a furious campaign to break the racial discrimination of sixty years and have a black captain of the West Indies cricket team, Frank Worrell, who later took over the captaincy to tour Australia that year.

James describes the details of the to and fro of play and the nuances and subtleties of a particular game on 30 January 1960 against the Marylebone Cricket Club (MCC), in the midst of these debates. The game saw a fairly typical change of fortune; it happens in cricket. Things can change very quickly and from being 22 for no wicket at close of play the previous evening, the West Indies collapsed and were soon 98 for 8. When Singh was dismissed by a run-out, the simmering anger of the spectators exploded. Such explosions are rare in cricket but James's account demonstrates: first, how much sport can matter; and second, how parallel and interconnected concerns about matters of sport and politics can become enmeshed.

Cricket is political with its legacy of colonialism, slavery and racialisation, which the Caribbean supporters carry along with their hopes of securing a national identity – and a black captain. As James writes:

> so there we are, all tangled up together, the old barriers breaking down and the new ones not yet established, a time of transition, always and inescapably turbulent. In the inevitable integration into a national community, one of the most urgent needs, sport and particularly cricket, has played and will play a great role. There is none in the West Indies who will not subscribe to the old aphorism 'What do they know of cricket who only cricket know?'
>
> *(James 2007:117)*

James is accounting for and explicating global forces that are condensed within the very local space of the cricket ground, with all its the personal and localised expressivities and intensities. These emotions are also embodied, as is so often the case in sporting discourses, into the persona of the captain and the players. The enfleshed selves of sport are also manifestations of its globalised capacities.

Sports heroes too can be reprised in the telling of their stories and can be made heroes retrospectively. For example, the story of Basil D'Oliviera, a cricketing hero who, at his death in 2011, was celebrated as having made a significant challenge to the apartheid regime in South Africa through cricket, is a case in point. D'Oliviera was the first black (in the apartheid regime classified as 'cape coloured') South African to play for an English county. An excellent all-rounder and high-scoring batsman, who, in spite of scoring 168 was only chosen to play for England in the tour to South Africa when another player Tom Cartwright, who had been chosen ahead of D'Oliviera, in spite of Dolly's most recent score of 168, dropped out. South Africa's response was to refuse to play a team with a black player in a climate of enormous hostility, which led to the most famous boycotts in sporting history and the long period of South Africa's isolation in international sport. When D'Oliviera died aged 83 in 2011, the obituaries and newspaper accounts expressed some of the tensions and guilt in the celebration of a great cricketer. Sports heroes can be reconfigured in the processes of remembering and move from carrying the status of the worthy and disadvantaged into more active heroic status. Once the apartheid regime had fallen in South Africa and Nelson Mandela had been released from prison, Mandela became a heroic figure even for those who had classified him as a criminal for his resistance to the regime before his imprisonment.

G/local sporting inequalities

Sport is localised in its affiliations and specificities as well as globalised in its politics and ever more so in a globalised economy, in its synergies with global media, broadcasting and sponsorship. Although sport is usually classified under the umbrella of culture, a consideration of global sport and the globalisation of sport makes it evident that sport is intensively political and embedded in economic systems as well as generating its own power mechanisms and social and economic processes. Sport is global, local and g/local; it is also intensely personal as well as collective in the passions it generates.

The much-vaunted mobilities of globalisation are evident in sport in its internationalism, including the transfer of players across the globe and especially in the speed of communication networks, but there have been significant impediments to these mobilities, especially through the mechanisms of racialised, ethnicised segregation that demonstrates the intersection of social, cultural and economic factors.

The intersection of local, specific situations with global opportunities operates in diverse ways, however. For example, the IOC's decision to include women's boxing as a sport in the 2012 games, the first time women have boxed at the games since 1904, when it was a demonstration sport, has coincided or maybe correlated with an increasing interest in the sport in Afghanistan. Twenty-six women from Afghanistan trained for the games in a climate that might have seemed incongruous, but the reasons they gave were very similar to those given by young men at the boxing gym, configured around self respect and improved self esteem through feeling good, about being able to 'look after yourself' and being in control of your own body.

The inclusion of women's boxing in the 2012 Games generated controversy, for example because of the reduction in the space for men's events arising from the advent of a 'new' sport. More troubling to many was the very existence of a sport for women, the purpose of which is to inflict damage on your opponent, that challenges traditional notions of gender. There are disjunctions between the public perception of boxing and the lived experience and even the recorded measurement of risk in the sport. According to an Australian survey in 1998, reported by Amateur International Boxing Association (AIBA), boxing came tenth in a league table of sporting injuries with rugby league well ahead, followed by sports such as rugby union, motorcycling, cricket and soccer. However sex gender permeates and shapes much of the debate and it may be the liberatory potential of boxing, especially in particular local contexts, that makes women's participation in the sport so threatening and so troubling.

One of main examples of the inclusion of women's boxing has been the interest in the sport in Muslim countries that are seen as characterised by such traditional sexual divisions. Nations deemed to be unlikely sources of women boxers, such as Afghanistan, have entered the ring. The contradictions of this phenomenon have not been lost on the media: Afghan women boxers train at a gym at the stadium formerly used by the Taliban for executions (including those of women convicted of adultery).

Boxing is not the only sport but it highlights how political transformations can be generated by sport. Embodied sporting practices, joining in, do not only represent resistance to social oppression and exclusion, but also they are materially part of the challenges to orthodoxy and part of the promise of sport on the global arena.

The idea of care of the self through diet and maintaining a healthy body through healthy living has been invoked in some discussion of men's boxing in Muslim societies but received little coverage in relation to women. The combination of anxiety about Islam in the west, which Muslims have had to negotiate in their daily lives, and excessive concerns with women's dress codes, put Islam and sport onto the agenda often in the media in terms of clothing and what would be appropriate dress for sporting activities. The modest dress approved by Islam is often far removed from the tight fitting sports clothing of many athletes on the world stage and even further removed from the sexualised Lycra skimpy garments of most women athletes in track and field events in the west. Concerns about dress do not always come from traditional religious leaders; FIFA attempted to stop Iranian Muslim women playing football by insisting the Iranian team conform to FIFA's dress code, thus intentionally or not fuelling the idea that for women to play football is for them to engage in a sexualised, immoral set of activities. Patriarchal practices are not exclusive to Islamic bodies. It is a messy business and demonstrates some of the tensions and contradictions in sport, but sport offers opportunities for greater freedom and the promise of change through its embodied practices. Grass-roots engagement is becoming increasingly successful, for example, the new Muslim Women Sport Foundation (MWSF) includes *futsal* (indoor football) and the Exclusively Women's Basketball League (EWBL).

The endurances of global sport are the inequalities as well as the opportunities for more democratic participation. The widening scope for participation in the Olympics manifest in the numbers of nations that participate and the expansion of the number of sports that are included is counterbalanced by the persistence of racism and ethnicised, racialised exclusion and the reinstatement of patriarchy as a major organising principle of sport. Racialisation and ethnicisation cannot be resolved through the visibility of more local campaigns such as Kick it Out (initially called the Kick Racism Out of Football Campaign) (KIO, 2011), although these play an important role in grass-roots activism and provide a trigger for change and also demonstrate the mix of local and the global and thus the g/local impact of sport. Racism endures in the continuation of racialised exclusions, whether from the upper echelons (any echelons?) of the regulatory bodies of global sport and even the continued white dominance of teams such as the South African cricket team, long after the demise of apartheid. It is not only about the empirical presence of black and ethnic minority people and women, it is about the values placed upon women's sport, the opportunities for visibility in the heroic narratives of sport as well as the limited sponsorship and support, for example, for women's sport. Economics and the flow of capital remain central to planet sport and inform its inequalities as well as the politics of its opportunities.

4

ECONOMIES OF SPORT

That sport is big business is unlikely to be disputed, but sports also operate in particular ways because of the merging of personal and collective passion with commercial possibilities and exploitations. Discourses of sport have also been underpinned by the negative associations of sporting success with money. There is often the implication that athletic activity and performance are somehow tainted and discredited by cash incentives. These assumptions are tied up with heroic narratives of sport as well as anxieties about corruption. To focus on the task in hand may also be good advice for embodied sporting practice rather than thinking about the rewards of victory. As the great Czech distance runner, Emile Zatopek, who won the three gold medals for 5000 metres, 10,000 metres and the marathon, breaking the Olympic record at each at Helsinki in 1952, is quoted as saying:

> an athlete cannot run with money in his pockets. He must run with hope in his heart and dreams in his head.

Hopes and dreams are crucial but athletes need shoes, kit, resources to provide training, time and space, and sporting inequalities across the globe are reinforced by lack of resource. There are complex interrelationships between the properties of sport, to generate excitement and thus opportunities for display and entertainment, and the contradictions of applying market forces and the principles of the pursuit of profit to so everyday and enjoyable a set of activities that discourses of health and well being suggest are beneficial at all levels in routine ways.

Sport offers particular promise for commercial interventions because of its powerful emotive affiliations as well as its, albeit possibly less intense, links with health and well being. Not all sports attract the same interest or investment. The economics of sport is complex, uneven and often very inequitable. Some sports recruit more sponsorship and generate more income. Golf, especially the men's game in the US and in parts of Europe, is a good example of a sport that is deeply embedded in commercial networks and, also because of the specificities of the game and where it is played (at sites that occupy extensive areas of land and with expensive equipment), considerable inequalities. Rankings, for example, in international men's golf are based on the amount of prize money that has been won; the last put in a competition is called the money shot, as when Luke Donald won two money titles in 2011 after his success in the Professional Golf Association (PGA) and the European Tour.

Flows of capital have been transformed by the political processes of globalisation and the political and economic systems that connect in new ways in the twenty-first century. In the case of the UK men's football league, the recent trend towards foreign takeovers of Premiership clubs, including buyers from Russia and the US, has made the front pages and the business and finance pages of the newspapers. Decisions about a UK club with strong traditions of local support are reported to have been made in a Texas court in the case of the sale of Liverpool Football Club in 2010. Not only are the club's players predominantly being drawn from across the globe, but also there has been much more debate about the solvency of international buyers than about on-pitch tactics.

The contradictions between global finance and local identifications and between global commercialised fandom and local resistance are well illustrated in the case of the Premiership, which also highlights some of the inequalities of sporting sponsorship. Not only have the top clubs in the Premiership received huge investments of overseas finance, along with incurring enormous debt, but other elements in the game have suffered because, for example, lower league clubs cannot compete in buying multimillion pound players, which renders the sport very unequal. The more expensive the players, the more chance there is of winning and the higher the rewards for broadcast rights and sponsorship. The women's game receives very little support with capital flows all being into the men's game. Gender inequalities are powerfully shaped by unequal resources as well as by different sets of rules and prescribed body practices on the field of play.

Gender inequalities play out in the Premiership and the Football Association (FA) and FIFA illustrate gender inequalities particularly clearly, especially in relation to the ways in which sports, including football, are sponsored and funded, which are inextricably linked to other aspects of social exclusion, for example those based on race, ethnicity, social class and disability. Generation has different implications in sport because the centrality of corporeality and the primacy afforded to body capacities means that youth, with its physical advantages of strength, stamina and speed, is rewarded. Inequalities operate differently in the bodies that regulate and monitor sport. In the case of media networks and especially organising bodies of sport, bodies are dominated by a patriarchy of older men, whereas it is youth that rules sporting practices in terms of financial remuneration as well as public presence, especially at elite levels of competition.

The Olympic Games present a particularly powerful illustration of the sports media sponsorship nexus in which economic factors are predominant. There are pivotal moments, for example in the bidding process to host the games, as hosting so massive a sporting event has huge implications for infrastructure investment and for possibilities of profit and loss, which is so often the case for the host city if not for its commercial investors (Gold and Gold, 2008; Horne, 2006; Preuss, 2006). At such times, sport is more likely to occupy the financial pages and websites than the back pages and sports-specific ones. The highly regarded *Financial Times* (FT), which provides global business coverage and includes comprehensive market intelligence, has no sports pages or supplements but, for example, the paper had 2,697 articles on the Olympics in thirty days in the autumn of 2011. There may be no scores or match schedules, beyond news of a big sporting moment, such as the outcome of international events such as the Olympics, the men's football World Cup or a cricket test series, but the FT has devoted considerable space to the financial and economic implications of the 2012 games and the categories of sporting records, which are based on financial investment returns and the position of sport in global economics. The FT version of keeping on track includes data such as the £11.5 million the British Olympic Association (BOA) needs to break even each year, the £13 million cost of funding the 550 Team GB athletes and the massive £376 million that is the combined funding for the other Olympic bodies. Investment responsibilities and possibilities are never far from what matters; for example BOA owns the exclusive rights to the Olympic branding from 2013 to 2016 (FT, 4 October 2011).

Money matters within sport as well as in the assemblages of finance, economy, politics and culture with which sporting practices intersect. There is a massive gap between the highly paid sports celebrities and megastars of the Premiership, the National Basketball Association (NBA), Major League Baseball (MLB) and both supporters and practitioners at other levels of engagement as well as the network of those who work in sport. Other networks operate in sport, which create marginalisation, such as the hegemonic masculinity that is so enduring in sport, so that the opportunities for financial reward for athletes, trainers, coaches, sports bodies and sponsors, whether through prize money, advertising revenue and wider possibilities for profit, coexist uncomfortably with policies and practices that promote wider participation and social inclusion. Sport cohabits with the networks of globalised hegemonic masculinity quite comfortably, although there have been disruptions and challenges to ubiquitous practices of hospitality, such as lavish entertaining and tickets for prestigious events as well as access to tournaments and clubs, including golf clubs, which have been notoriously slow to embrace sex equality in some parts of the world.

One of the effects of sport has been to contribute to the escalation of fast-flowing market forces in global economies. Sport offers opportunities for investment that is psychic and financial, although the confluence of these two elements has provoked debate about the authenticity of fandom and the fair-weather commitments of investors, managers and players. At points it is difficult to disentangle or assess the feelings of fans and financial investors because big business is such a feature of contemporary social and sporting life.

One example of these points of connection and merging is the case of higher education in the US where university finance depends heavily on sports sponsorship. When the Pennsylvania State University coach was dismissed for allegedly committing acts of sexual assault against boys over a period of thirteen years, the riot it provoked was due more to the coach's dismissal than moral outrage at the allegations of the cover-up by the college hierarchy. It appears that football alone generated $50.4 million profit for the university in the 2009–10 academic year. What makes the phenomenon, which is far from unique, particularly pertinent to a discussion of social change and the relationship between sport and other social forces, divisions and relations is the ways in which athletics and sporting practices can become so central to the life of other institutions, including the academy. Sport provides mechanisms for securing relationships, social inclusions and exclusions in a manner that other cultural practices cannot emulate, although religious belonging can offer some possibilities. Economics and sport are more firmly connected, however. Sport provides positive connections between people and communities, but it can also reinstate racialised, ethnicised, class-based networks, and most notably those of hegemonic masculinity.

These current trends resonate with elements in the genealogy of sport. There have always been connections between economics and sport. Sport is not and never has been a cash- or reward-free space. Sport is constituted by histories that demonstrate the powerful links between commercial and financial interests and those of play and embodied sporting practices that include betting on the outcomes. What is called sport is strongly connected to engaging in particular bodily practices and sporting activities that range from field sports such as shooting, hunting and fishing, where there is reward in terms of rewards that can be consumed or sold, to boxing for financial reward, whether through gambling on outcomes or prize money. It is a complex mix, and modern sport and even pre-modern sport have never been only about play without any financial incentives. Postmodern sport, including alternative and extreme sport, may offer some challenges to financial incentives, but challenges and resistance often operate in relation to the economic deprivation that can limit opportunities and create exclusivity and social exclusion from full participation in mainstream sport. Sport has always offered the possibility of escape, notably in the heroic boxing narratives of the escape from the ghetto and achievement of financial success and security. Other challenges might come from contemporary body projects and engagements with promoting personal well being through engaging in playful sporting activities, but these practices too are located within an economy of privilege that permits some the leisure to so indulge themselves. There is not a linear narrative from playful engagement to highly competitive, remunerative, professional elite sport.

The dominance of market forces and the pursuit of profit are challenged, however, and this is manifest in some of the changes that are being made in US universities. It is possible to recognise the value of sport in higher education and to acknowledge the changing cultures in which universities have to access the funding and resource that sport can provide without resorting to traditional repressive regimes of social exclusion and privilege. The emergence of scandals onto the public agenda, however, makes it possible to challenge excess, and alternatives become thinkable.

One aspect of economics, or more specifically finance, that operates within a framework of ethical discourses, is the relationship between professional and amateur athletes, none more so than in the Olympics, which remain haunted by the ghosts of nineteenth-century gentlemanly amateurism for athletes and governing bodies.

Ethics permeates the discourse of sport, in myriad forms: the ethics of fair play on and off the pitch; as part of sport's heroic narratives and the logic of good versus evil in which cheating should have no part. Modern sport is also a set of very highly regulated and disciplined practices that demand compliance and yet invite contradiction. It is hardly surprising that sport speaks so volubly of equity and justice framed by impartiality; each game even has its own arbiter in the form of at least one referee or umpire. Umpiring decisions rarely occupy a neutral space but are mostly interpreted within a frame of justice and morality, which is also to be expected given the partisan nature of spectatorship and supporter affiliations as well as the powerful financial incentives to win, especially in elite sport. Golf is largely played without an umpire, but as the Royal and Ancient guidelines suggest:

> All players should conduct themselves in a disciplined
> manner, demonstrating courtesy and sportsmanship at all
> times, irrespective of how competitive they may be. Eti-
> quette is an integral and inextricable part of the game,
> which has come to define golf's values worldwide.
>
> *(Royal and Ancient, 2011)*

Nineteenth-century notions of fair play accompanied by the cult
of the gentlemanly amateur seem a long way from contemporary
sporting practices.

The late nineteenth-century recovery of the Olympics and the
renaissance of Olympism invoked the idea of amateurism
and constructed ethical sport as that which was undertaken in
the spirit of the game and not for reward. This entailed
some rewriting of the Ancient games for which prizes were
awarded and the patronage of young male athletes by older
men yielded a range of rewards. What is significant about
the debates in sport that invoke the higher moral ground of
amateurism are the ways in which contingent social and
political values in sport and the wider social terrain are co constitutive. Sport provides us with the language of heroism and
moral rectitude and reinforces what are usually gendered ethical
codes.

What has been read as the overt idealism of the founders of
the modern Games and commonly attributed to de Coubertin as
a man who opposed athletics as professional display, would lead
to commercially based large-scale events, which would corrupt
the amateur spirit of the Olympics. De Coubertin's acclaimed
idealism might have been construed as naïve optimism, although
it is also historically and discursively situated as one of the regulatory mechanisms in play in the nineteenth and early twentieth
centuries. The disavowal of commercialism, made explicit in de
Coubertin's statements, is also part of a nineteenth-century moral
and religious regime of truth that located commerce and morality as contradictory mechanisms.

Amateurism is a male version of white, middle-class, female morality as embodied in the idea of the Victorian poet Coventry Patmore's (2012 [1867]) *Angel in the House*, who, as the model of moral femininity, is the guardian of morality in the Victorian household, responsible for the excesses of the pursuit of profit by men in the public arena of capitalist endeavour. The separation of commerce and trade from morality and high mindedness was familiar rhetoric within the discursive regimes of the bourgeoisie. In the case of masculinity, the discursive field of play is commerce, where greed must be regulated and policed. Femininity carried the responsibility for controlling, moderating and containing male sexuality and its excesses, largely through being kept in ignorance, but nevertheless within a framework of morality. In sport this was also class based, with gentlemen who did not need to participate for money being best placed to make decisions about the regulation and structure of sport.

The all but abandonment of the amateur ideal and of the amateur–professional division is one that might carry some equitable connotations as well as being steeped in commercialised pursuit of profit and individualised greed. The amateur–professional divide and transgressions of the boundary between the two is not uniform across all sports, although amateur status is increasingly difficult to define. For example the games have always provided a route into professional status for boxers and there is a star-studded history of great boxers who followed this route, not least Muhammad Ali himself who won gold in Rome in 1960.

Financial and economic forces have always played a key role in sport. Although sport reflects economic transformations historically. Industrialisation influenced the first professional sports leagues and post industrialisation has been strongly implicated in the media sponsorship nexus through which mega leagues have developed in men's sport, especially in the twenty-first century. There are also specificities in sport that influence the intersections of commercial and media forces of power and generate

particular interventions and practices, notably in relation to the
capacities of sport to generate passionate commitments and the
exhilaration of embodied activities and the risks and dangers of
participation and spectatorship. Some stakeholders have benefited
and these developments have created new stakeholders, media
networks, broadcast services, promoters, agents and notably a
new class of sports stars, a relatively small number of whom earn
massive fees not only for their performance on the field but also
in the commercial synergies created by the sport media nexus
and expansion of sites for the purveyance of popular cultural
products. Such benefits have increasingly been concentrated for
example on the celebrity stars, mega leagues and top clubs
through sponsorship deals. Many have not benefited, notably the
focus and site of the channelling of resource has been in men's
sport while women's teams and clubs struggle to gain any sponsorship. Global inequalities mean that resources are distributed
according to the rationality on irrationality of market forces,
which again lead to particular emphasis on sports such as the
men's big team games. Fans are charged increasingly high gate
prices and there are movements of resistance to the takeover of
clubs, for example in men's football by foreign buyers who also
bring with them enormous debts; FC United has had some
success in its challenge to the Glazers' takeover of Manchester
United by setting up a fan-run club. Manchester City, although
occupying a seemingly secure place at the top of the Premiership, has not seen any such successful resistance, but the picture is
complex and sport still offers opportunities. The media commerce sport nexus is dynamic and there are always gaps, shifts
and possibilities in sport. It is not only played at the mega-event
level.

The economics of sport has created branches of medicine and
physiotherapy and training programmes that have wider applications. The pharmaceutical industry has a sometimes troubling
and mostly ambivalent relationship with sport, but it may be the
promise of the future, however, and the ethical debates about

which interventions are permissible and which are not, for example in the case of disabled athletes with prostheses as well as the use of performance enhancing drugs, may become redundant.

Money makes the possibility of the mega event and the spectacle, but the commercialisation of sport can also threaten as well as promise, and the spectacles of practised sport can be damaging as well as entertaining. Such events can provide opportunities for corruption as well as celebration, but the spectacle, the spectacular as well as the sensational and what makes up sensation are a key part of planet sport.

5

BOUNDARIES OF CERTAINTY

Sport is a field where records and measurement count. It matters that times and speeds are accurately measured in athletics, especially given the high rewards that are now involved. Other sports demand visualisation and filming techniques and heat-sensitive equipment as well as additional human resources; cameras at the wicket in cricket, at the touch line in rugby to adjudicate tries amidst an ever more voluble demand for more and more accuracy to judge outcomes, ensure fair play and redress the inadequacies of the human eye and the lack of all-round vision of the referee. Technologies are constantly developing more sensitive and precise means of ensuring accuracy to ever-higher standards of precision. These developments are inspired by the expanding technoscience that is the motor to much sporting innovation and the quest for certainty.

Certainties are interpreted in different ways in particular sports but these developments are all framed by the expectation that sport is a set of activities that can be accurately measured and about which there can be a high degree of certainty, especially given modern technologies. Pharmaceutical companies are developing more complex drugs, for example, that can be used to mask the effects of the performance-enhancing drug taken in the first place. The regulatory bodies of sport such as the IOC and IAAF, in spite of their global reach, cannot keep up with the market-led advances with which the drug companies are engaged. There are tensions between, on the one hand, the movement for ever more vigilant monitoring and brave, idealist attempts to eliminate what is construed as cheating and, on the other hand, the recognition that all elite athletes are involved in a highly sophisticated programme of enhancement through nutrition, training that is physical and psychological and a panoply of interventions that defy the attempts of the regulatory bodies of sport and blur the boundaries of legality. Sport is not a fair playing field.

The search for certainty and truth also targets the bodies of athletes, notably in relation to sex gender, because in sport there are two sexes whatever the ambiguities in the wider cultural terrain of contemporary life, and in terms of performance enhancement by whatever means, but mostly pharmaceutical. The other area of concern that is closely linked to the matter of performance enhancement in this quest is the evaluation of the disabled or able-bodied athlete; an area in which technological advance has created more not less uncertainty.

In the context of sex gender, certainty is to be achieved through what is now called gender verification. Gender verification tests happen regularly at the Olympics and it is universally a test carried out on women; there is always the suspicion that a woman who performs to a very high standard or has the musculature or body attributes of masculinity might be a man who is cheating. One of the most controversial recent cases was that of Caster Semenya, the South African 800-metre runner.

In August 2009 the Berlin World Athletics Championships were shaken by controversy. Caster Semenya, an 18-year-old from South Africa, won the 800-metre title by nearly 2.5 seconds, finishing in 1:55.45. Only 3 hours after winning the gold medal, Caster was at the centre of a harsh, very public contestation concerning her gender. A bitterly disappointed Italian runner, Elisa Cusma, who finished sixth, was reported as saying that Caster was really a man. Cusma was not the only confused commentator on the case, as is evident in the enormous coverage given to the 800-metre gold medallist Caster Semenya. She was fast, so fast that other athletes questioned whether she was a woman, leading the IAAF to instigate gender verification tests, albeit in a procedure that, contrary to guidelines, was leaked before the final at the World Athletics Championships in August 2009. The case started badly with the victory of the athlete being so quickly followed by this procedural offence by the IAAF in disclosing information about the tests prior to the results. Perhaps ironically, Caster Semenya did not break the 800-metre record of 1:53.28 that had been set by the Czech athlete Jarmila Kratochvila in 1983. Kratochvila too had been subjected to chromosomal sex testing at the Olympics in 1980 on grounds of her strongly muscled shoulders, arms and thighs. There are significant endurances in the experience of women athletes, although the Semenya case achieved considerable significance because of the volubility and visibility of the debate and its condensation of so many diverse factors.

Women athletes have to reassure us of their femininity, through comportment (Young, 2005) and appearance, even when they, through the body practices of their sport, necessarily have very different bodies from their female non-sporting counterparts. Public debate is always framed by a moral discourse of 'fair play' that invokes the unfair advantage that men who pass as women might gain in sport, but what is most alarming and distressing about these cases is the humiliation that women undergo in being subjected to 'verification' and the public and expert scrutiny that is reserved for women, and detracts from celebratory possibilities of the achievements of elite women athletes.

The Caster Semenya case was itself transformative, however, and generated affects that led to shifts in public opinion that differed markedly from the early reactions to the case. Change included the incorporation of the dimensions of the politics of race and ethnicity into the case, especially in discussion of the responses of the South African government and South African sports bodies. By 2011 it was very different and there was at least acknowledgement of how badly Caster had been treated. The BBC commissioned a television programme that gave some voice to the lived experience of the athlete and her family (BBC, 2011). The programme was framed by the phenomenology of lived experience and recounted not only the details of Caster's experience of her sport but also her life in South Africa and the expectations and assumptions of her friends and family. The programme revisited the narrative of Caster's ban from athletics competitions and related the story of the role of the IAAF and Athletics South Africa (ASA) and the subsequent battle for her reinstatement, which was eventually announced on 6 July 2010.

Caster's case has not been the only one. There have been eight since 2005, but Caster's experience served as a test case and assumed the status of global visibility as well as bringing together so many different aspects of the inequalities of sport, including not only sex gender as the immediate focus, but also race and the inequalities of global power geometries of poverty as exemplified by Caster's own family background in South Africa.

Whereas certainties about sex gender are usually situated within powerfully entrenched traditions and appeals to the longevity and universalism of the dual categories of female and male, upon which contemporary science can elaborate with some detail, other categories of person are more problematic; the question of disabled sports presents a more complex problem. In the Olympics, disabled athletes have to achieve specific minimum standards of performance. The Paralympics present a compromise solution achieved by the efforts of the disability sports movement. This is another binary logic that appears to divide human beings into disabled and able-bodied, but the relationship between the two movements remains contested and the dividing lines between disabled and the able-bodied have become ever more difficult to determine with embodiment at the centre of the political debate.

The case of Oscar Pistorius raises questions about the nature of certainties that appeal to technologies of scientific expertise that are implicated in the change which the regulatory bodies of sport have to address. These attempts at finding the truth are relevant to the discussion of sex gender and in particular gender verification testing. The South African runner Oscar Pistorius, whose science-fiction epithet, Blade Runner, derives from the cheetah flex-foot blades that enable him to run very fast, is a double amputee with highly specialised state-of-the-art carbon-fibre prosthetic limbs. He won the right to compete in the Olympics at Beijing and to compete against able-bodied athletes, even though he had hitherto competed only in the competitions for athletes with disabilities, having been disqualified from able-bodied athletics meetings by the IAAF because his prosthetics qualified as technical aids. In the end, Pistorius failed to qualify for the Olympics and ran in the Paralympics, but his case raises several questions about the classificatory systems of sport and the measurement processes through which categories might be secured, whether of dis/ability or sex gender.

First, the promise of the objective certainties of technology are, at least partly, subordinate to other materialities, notably the social and the economic. In the intersection of power axes, there remains a hierarchical weighting that challenges the fluidity of the systems within this assemblage and reaffirms elements of a more-determinist paradigm. Pistorius was only able to access such superior technology as an affluent white, male South African.

Second, technologies offer possibilities that transcend an essentialist notion of embodiment, but the body is inextricably implicated in the constitutive aspects of subjectivity and retains some of the limitations of corporeality. Technological advances may produce an enhancement of capabilities, but they disrupt certainties, transgress boundaries and do not necessarily offer criteria for measurement and evaluation which could then secure knowledge. Without underplaying the massive advances of technology and science and their liberating potential for bodies that are impaired, damaged, frail or sick, it might be possible to overstate the guarantees technoscience might offer for evaluating its own success or its own outcomes. In the case of Pistorius, as an example of setting the boundaries around disability and able-bodiedness and deciding what constitutes corporeal perfor-mance enhancement, there is also the problem of essentialism.

Third, arising from the ghost of essentialist certainties, the Blade Runner example poses a question about the classification of difference and how it is constituted, if, indeed, the concept still has any purchase in the search for certainty. It has been suggested that boundaries are so blurred that there should be no restrictions on the level of assistance or enhancement, although this might lead to the absurd possibility that able-bodied athletes would seek amputation of their limbs if the prostheses they could use would render them even faster than their able-bodied counterparts.

The sex gender binary of female and male is deeply embedded in discussion of truth and authenticity and invokes a certainty and authenticity that scientific verification principles might guarantee. Science is the resource for guidance with the objec-tivism to inform a series of tests that could bestow certainty. The binary logic of the system posits two bounded categories of sex based upon genetic, anatomical criteria, which if correctly applied following prescribed procedures could determine to which sex a person belongs. Sex, however, is too messy even in sport to be susceptible to the application of simple criteria of assessment, or even the increasingly complex criteria that have been developed in gender verification tests. A proliferation of categories of expertise or of sex gender does not in itself address fluidity or break down boundaries; more expert witnesses may merely create more boundaries. Sex gender seems to defy regulatory mechanisms designed to fit people neatly into pregiven sexes; the criteria that have been developed are not fit for purpose and are addressing the wrong questions in seeking medical, scientific certainties.

It is not only a matter of people deciding for themselves what sex they are, sex is enfleshed and lived and the sexed self is situated within a gendered social world where sex matters. Empirically, the majority of people live their lives as female or male and there are enfleshed differences that contribute to the classificatory system that is in place, but that is nonetheless contingent and culturally specific within discursive regimes (Foucault, 1981).

Flesh is implicated in sex gender and how it is understood, represented and experienced. The concept of being enfleshed offers a way of acknowledging and embracing commonalities among people, as well, of course, as between humans and non humans, whether in relationships between species or between animate and inanimate matter (Haraway, 2003), for example, as in the case of disabled athletes and the use of prostheses, other forms of matter can substitute for and act as flesh.

There is some confusion between philosophical and empirical categories of sex gender that could be clarified by exploring some of the specificities of lived experiences and the plasticity of flesh, by combining flesh and experience, perception of self with the perception of others and of situating enfleshed selves within the social world.

Material bodies are the target of sporting practice and the subjects of sporting success and celebration, but they are also troubling and troubled by the gender binary that underpins all sporting practice. There are anatomical, corporeal differences between women and men as well as cultural differences. Whilst these may be recognised by a feminist politics of difference, it is often only particular differences that become the focus of attention within sport. Social construction can overemphasise the plasticity of bodies and, by concentrating upon the body as socially inscribed, may miss the inequalities that are in play. Sex rather than gender may offer more purchase for embracing difference whilst highlighting sources of inequality and the material operation of power. Sex has to acknowledge the potential of transformation through embodied practices and their intersection with the materialities that include culture class, race, ethnicity and the technologies through which changes take place.

Gender is also tied up with compulsory heterosexuality and although sex and sexuality are not synonymous, there are points of connection and synergies that are productive in focusing upon sex as a key concept in explaining inequalities and women's experience of sport and its practices.

The IOC and other sports bodies were so alarmed at the plasticity of flesh and the transformations in women's bodies through elite sport that the tests could have been seen as offering reassurance that heterosexual normativity was secure and that it could be secured. Even into the twenty-first century, as the case of Caster Semenya shows, for a woman to challenge patriarchal norms and the gendered sexual attractiveness of the heterosexual matrix, is much too subversive to be tolerated. A woman athlete, who as an enfleshed being has the capacity for speed, does not receive the acclaim of male elite athletes; she is suspect because her performance challenges the hegemony of masculinity in sport and because subversion of the rigidity of the sex gender binary is too troubling and unsettling as it defies the certitudes of truth and the reliability of verification. Men are subject to testing too of course but the rigours of science and technology are applied in cases of disabled athletes or when performance enhancement is involved.

Although the introduction of gender verification testing at the Olympics was intended to prevent men from competing as women, such tests also serve to reinstate patriarchy, ethnocentricity, normative heterosexuality and nationalism. It is noteworthy that the tests were called gender rather than sex verification. It is contradictory given the scientific, objectivist approach taken by the regulatory bodies of sport, such as the IOC, that the organising body should have opted for the more culturally inflected term, rather than a more biological version of the sex. The aim may have been to create a more comprehensive version of proof that took on board the cultural and social and psychological dimensions of being female or male, which gender was seen as more likely than sex to deliver. The cultural practices of athletes and their visible appearance certainly play a large part in decisions about who was to be tested; a masculine comportment and outward appearance suggest the need for proof that this person is a woman and not a man. Science and technoscience generate as many, if not more, uncertainties as they purport to clarify in the regimes of truth that encompass and recreate sex gender.

Sex gender is central to sport and one of the axes of power that intersects with other axes of power through which social relations and inequalities are forged and identifications made by enfleshed selves. Sex connects to other materialities such as wealth and poverty, race and place. The example of Caster Semenya's experience highlights the centrality of racialisation, which is spatially and temporally inflected, in these debates about gender verification, where science meets sex, race and ethical judgements.

The search for certainty in sport has entered muddy waters, but by looking at how the regulatory bodies deal with uncertainties it is possible to extrapolate some of the elements that make up differences and inequalities and processes of classification that operate more broadly as well as how they are enacted in everyday life.

6

EVERYDAY ROUTINES

The ordinary affects of sport

Involvement with sport includes a range of embodied practices –
on the pitch and in the gym as well as through the practices
of spectatorship. The connections between the public display of
sport and the intensities of sporting experience and everyday
routines raise questions about how spectatorship is also routine
and iterative. Boundaries are blurred between the authenticities
of fandom; being there at every game still carries weight
but there are other ways of expressing support and solidarity,
especially in the context of ever-changing media–commerce
intersections in which communication systems, fast developing
Internet and satellite technologies are in play.

Mega events and the lives of sports superstars invade personal
lives and new technologies permit the transmission of sporting
events not only across the globe but in local spaces where the
big-screen satellite viewing, for example in a public square, at a
local sports club or bar, generates camaraderie as well as a better
view of the game. In many sports, such as football, baseball and
boxing, there are discourses of authenticity that suggest that

being present at the game has more validity in the construction of fan identities than watching from a distance – increasingly a possibility for people across the globe through technological developments. However, participating in sport includes routine encounters, expressions of solidarity and camaraderie, shared exchanges, reflections and debates and myriad ordinary acts, some of which actually constitute doing sport in informal settings, such as on the beach, in the park or on the street as well as in more formal situations such as the gym, the sports centre, training ground or club. Following sport, engaging routinely with the vicissitudes of being involved as a follower as well as taking part in everyday embodied sporting practices are all part of the field of sport and the processes through which sport matters.

The everyday is imbricated in the more public arenas of sport and there are diverse points of connection within the field of sport.

Everyday fandom

Different sports recruit participants and followers for a variety of reasons. This can be in relation to the desire to follow a celebrity player. Boxers regularly cite a famous boxer as their inspiration for engaging in the sport. Muhammad Ali has inspired millions (Marqusee, 2005; Hauser, 1991) as did Mike Tyson, however controversial a figure he became (O'Connor, 2002). In the gym boxers also cite a family member or local hero. Johnny Nelson, former WBO cruiser-weight champion, says it was his brother who inspired him (Woodward, 2006). In some sports it may be a family tradition, spatially located, or peer groups, initially at school or in adolescence, that create and support interest in sport and its allegiances.

Why does sport generate such powerful commitment? Support for a particular club is avowedly not rational. Football fans acknowledge that the rational decision would be to be a fair-weather supporter of, for example one of the top Premiership clubs – a view that is shared by many who follow one of the big men's team games across the globe. Rationality is not central to sporting identifications, however, although fans do rationalise their sense of belonging and familial bonds are often cited. I support Sheffield Wednesday football club in Yorkshire in the UK where we have lived for most of my adult life. Because three of my four children so enthusiastically espoused the club when they first went to school, I find the sense of belonging replicates some of the intensities of connection and memories of everyday family exchanges and, of course trips to Hillsborough, the club ground.

Followers of sport also recognise that it is the embodied activities on the pitch that create and inspire these strong identifications, as expressed by fans of Barnsley Town, a Championship English football club (a club that is, at the time of writing, playing in the second division of the four league Premiership; it has a long tradition and has played in the top league but is not world ranking or rich):

> I love watching the lads passing it around instead of using the long ball method ... the lows are watching a poor performance.
>
> *(Hadfield, 2010)*

The flows and mobilities of sport that are part of the visual display at the ground and the sounds and rhythms of commentary at a distance create and sustain the identifications of followers.

Failure to win, and especially relegation, is likely to be the cause of negative feelings but is certainly not a reason to abandon allegiance to the club. Loss intensifies the emotional affects of sport. As one fan says, it has been 'a rollercoaster of a ride for the best part of 60 years but I wouldn't have missed it'. Fans speak of the kinship ties, most commonly through the male line, which bind them to a club: 'I was there with my son. I cried. I wish my dad could have been there' (Hadfield, 2010), which translates the affective bonds of family into the emotion of fandom.

Sport offers a space in which it is possible and even acceptable for grown men with strong investments in hegemonic masculinity to cry and to display emotion. Sport generates affects that are emotional and material in contradictory ways. Along with the routine acceptance of emotional affects is also the everyday violence that can erupt after games. These are the ordinary affects within the global framework of sport (Stewart, 2007). The enforcement of strong policing and the promotion of policies of social cohesion have reduced such displays at the ground, especially in football, but some of the violence has been displaced to other sites, either in the streets between groups of opposing fans or, as often happens after major international events, such as the men's football World Cup, domestic violence. Sport, even in its routine practices, is contradictory. Its affects cross the boundaries between public and private spheres and between different relationships including those of intimacy, friendship, kinship and community.

Points of connection are central to the routine affiliations of sport as well as the big moments of belonging and the imagined communities of mega events. In the field of sport there are also powerful embodied connections, among participants, fans at the game or watching at home or in a community. One of the under-explored synergies is between those who commentate and those who research sport and the field of research. Whilst journalists are more explicitly caught up in the networks of hegemonic masculinity through hospitality events and hosted dinners for example, sports researchers who adopt qualitative research methods, might appear to take the role of outsiders, especially in retaining some sense of objective distance in interpreting and understanding the field of research.

How can you access the ordinary affects and routines of sport?

Phenomenology of the everyday

In order to access the everyday routines of embodied sporting, researchers have been drawn to phenomenology and to ethnographic methodologies that include participant observation. Phenomenology is particularly attractive in sport research because it permits engagement with the embodiment and embodied selves that are so central to sport and a focus upon the lived experience of practitioners and participants and their accounts of 'being in the world'. Such approaches also have the advantage of enabling the researcher to access the everyday social worlds by permitting the subjects of research to speak for themselves. Phenomenological approaches, for example drawing upon Bourdieu's use of Merleau-Ponty (1962) allow entry into a social world in which people talk about either their allegiances or what they actually do in sport, the embodied practices and how sport is 'in their blood'. In order to be immersed in the field and to generate these accounts, some collusion is required. Allied to the tendency of phenomenological approaches towards being more descriptive and relatively uncritical, the approach does have limitations. The acceptance of the subjects' accounts as transparent reflections or representations of their experience may also invite the collusion of insider status, which in sport can lead to a reiteration of hegemonic masculinities.

Sport also attracts researchers who already have some affiliations to the field and its culture and the field is marked by collusions, notably with the hegemonic masculinity that pervades the routine iterative practices of sport. As Connell (1995) argues so persuasively, what makes hegemonic masculinity so strongly implicated in such diverse social worlds is its exclusions and the networks of inclusions it generates that extend beyond those who embody traditional enfleshed masculinity. Sports such as Australian rules football, boxing and baseball generate commitment and personal and collective psychic investments by those who themselves lack the capacities to engage in the body practices of the sport, but nonetheless lay claim to the properties of the traditional, muscular, heroic, strong, aggressive masculinities by association: they can talk the talk and witness, for example the more brutal practices of boxing without flinching. This is particularly relevant in sport. It is more marked in some sports than others of course. For example, the collusions and collaborations of hegemonic masculinity in boxing extend far beyond the boxers themselves to embrace not only the fans and followers but more especially the journalists, commentators and sometimes researchers.

However, in sport immersion and observing participation can deliver insights into the routine, iterative body practices that are so central to the field.

WacQuant demonstrates from his own experience as an apprentice boxer and temporary immersion in the field that pugilism and, in particular, the pugilistic habitus, are achieved through routine body practices of training and sparring. A boxer's moves:

> Far from being 'natural' and self-evident, the basic punches (left jab, right hook, right cross, straight right hand and uppercut) are difficult to exercise properly and presuppose a thorough 'physical rehabilitation,' a genuine remoulding of one's kinetic coordination, and even a psychic conversion. It is one thing to visualize and to understand them in thought, quite another to realize them and, even more so, to combine them in the heat of action … Theoretical mastery is of little help … and it is only after it has been assimilated by the body in and through endless physical drills repeated *ad nauseam* that it becomes in turn fully intelligible to the intellect. There is indeed a comprehension of the body that goes beyond – and comes prior to – full visual and mental cognizance.
>
> *(WacQuant, 2004:69)*

The immersion of what WacQuant (2004) calls the 'observing participant' may invoke, on the one hand, a perspective that is taken from the subjective position of the researcher and may therefore lack distance, or on the other hand, may provide deeper insights that enrich the findings and create a more accurate picture of the field. Boxing presents a particular site that is strongly configured around gender polarities. The researcher is not only inside the field as a participant, he is also colluding with a particular version of masculinity. As Judith Butler (1990, 1993) argues, although not in any way connected to sport, one does not have to be classified as male to 'do masculinity' because sex, like gender is a set of iterative practices that themselves generate the classification. There are, however, consistencies and endurances in the social, material and cultural barriers that make it difficult for women to perform masculinity, especially in the field of sport. There are enfleshed differences that matter in this field, which render the women who 'do masculinity' parodic in a sense that lacks any of the political force Butler attributes to transgression and the parodic. In a sport such as boxing, parody is more likely to be translated into the manner in which Joyce Carol Oates (1987) attributes the parodic to women boxers as not the real thing; women are parodies of men who are the real thing. What this demonstrates is that this is not a level playing field and the enfleshed materialities combine with social and cultural forces in particular ways that can reinstate inequalities as well as at other times providing opportunities.

Ethnography privileges the insider, placing the male researcher in boxing within a twenty-first century rearticulation of the Fancy, privy to disclosures about associated everyday activities, outside the ring and the gym, such as gambling, dog fighting and, in some cases, bare-knuckle fighting. However, these practices and networks are very specifically gendered, in ways that are not always acknowledged (Woodward, 2009).

This discussion also raises questions about women as researchers in traditionally masculine fields and the acknowledgement of sex gender difference. Women are always marked in sport, whatever role they play whereas, as has already been argued, men's sport is the norm that appears to be gender neutral, albeit whilst embedding traditional masculinities. These reflections are instructive in thinking about how what appear to be common-sense assumptions about physicality and embodiment and everyday differences are reproduced in sport, and sport is not merely a reflection of wider social and political forces and processes.

One of the problems with an account such as WacQuant's is that the researcher is complicit and insufficiently situated in relation to the field of research; disruption becomes imperceptible, if not impossible, in the smooth operation of the habitus.

Yvonne Lafferty and Jim McKay (2004), in their study of the interaction between Australian women and men boxers, draw upon WacQuant's interpretation of *illusio* as 'collective misrecognition' (WacQuant, 2001). WacQuant suggests that *illusio* is a means of demonstrating that boxers are not deceived by an exploitative system that compels them to sell their bodies to the pugilistic trade but that they are enmeshed in a powerful belief system that holds onto the honour and nobility of the sport, which is called the Noble Art. It is hard to see how women could be similarly implicated since the *doxa* of boxing is one that manifests little cultural tradition of women in kinship groups and social networks having boxing 'in their blood', although individual women may give voice to such commitment.

Phenomenological approaches to the relationship between material bodies and the lived experience of 'being in the world' are useful in accessing the everyday bodily practices of sport and especially in challenging the Cartesian binary of mind and body. For example WacQuant's discussion of illusion goes some way towards explaining elements of being in the zone (without the transcendent elements of excitement perhaps). It shows how everyday sporting practices work and the synergies between thought processes and body practices that make sport routine. One aspect that is underplayed is that of the relationship between the representations of sport and the wider terrain in which sport is made and remade, regulated and transformed.

One approach that has been influential in taking on board the social situatedness of the sporting body is Simone de Beauvoir's (1989 [1949]) conceptualisation of bodies as situations and situated bodies that, although she never had any interest in sport, does accommodate sex differences and a more dynamic approach to body practices and embodied selves. In sports studies there is, not surprisingly, a strong emphasis upon physicality and physiognomy, which, perhaps surprisingly, has only recently taken on board the differences of the sexed body in relation to medical treatment. There remains a separation between the realm of material bodies, flesh, bone, blood, muscle and skin that are the domain of medical science and the cultural and social realms of sport. There are, however, increasingly attempts to bring together the ways in which bodies and their social and cultural worlds intersect and de Beauvoir's work has been used to inform some more recent approaches to combining these elements.

Situated bodies; bodies as situations

The meanings of bodies are not written on the surface, nor will the experience be the same for everyone. Simone de Beauvoir suggests that the human body is ambiguous; subject to natural laws and to the human production of meaning:

> It is not merely as a body, but rather as a body subject to taboos, laws, that the subject becomes conscious of himself and attains fulfilment – it is with reference to certain values that he [sic] valorizes himself. To repeat once more: physiology cannot ground any values; rather, the facts of biology take on the values that the existent bestows upon them.
>
> *(de Beauvoir, 1989 [1949]:76)*

Bodies as represented, for example as marginalised, also experience themselves and are crucial to an understanding of self hood and the processes through which people position themselves and are positioned within the social world:

> The body is not a thing, it is a *situation* ... it is the instrument of our grasp upon the world, a limiting factor for projects.
>
> *(de Beauvoir, 1989 [1949]:66)*

This approach provides a way of bringing together the natural, material body, the experiences of embodied selves and the situations, which include representations, practices and policies, which recreate the lived body. Athletes, even those who only engage in informal sporting practices, are involved in some sort of body project that involves a degree of exertion and playing by the rules. De Beauvoir attributes more agency to the project than the situations in which most people find themselves. Bodies are not 'just' in a situation, nor are they just objects of empirical inquiry; bodies are more than this. De Beauvoir's analysis of the 'lived body' provides a means of enabling

> a situated way of seeing the subject based on the understanding that the most important location or situation is the roots of the subject in the spatial frame of the body.
>
> *(Braidotti, 1994:161)*

Bodies are situated on the margins through structural factors such as economic inequalities, racialisation, ethnicisation, discrimination on grounds of gender and of physical or mental impairment, but bodies are also themselves situations through which people experience themselves, both negatively and positively. As Toril Moi argues 'To claim that the body *is* a situation is not the same as to say that it is placed *within* some other situation. The body is both a situation and is placed within other situations' (Moi, 1999: 65).

Embodied selves, understood through the trope of lived bodies, accord greater agency and possibility for transformation than the social worlds in which sport is routinely experienced would permit. The approach is attractive in the field of sport, however, because it avoids the reduction of the self to the body by acknowledging both the situations that bodies inhabit and the interrelationship between bodies and situations. De Beauvoir argues that to claim that the body is a situation is to acknowledge that having a woman's body is bound up with the exercise of freedom. The body-in-the-world is in an intentional relationship with the world, although as Young (2005) argues, women do often end up living their bodies as things. Lived embodiment disrupts dichotomies of mind and body, nature and culture, public and private, and foregrounds experience (Young, 2005).

Young's feminist phenomenological approach, which deploys the concept of embodiment, attempts to redress the imbalance in Merleau-Ponty's work by focusing on gender and, in particular, the specificities of women's embodiment. Young challenges the universal account of the gender-neutral body implied by Merleau-Ponty and claims that the female body is not simply experienced as a direct communication with the active self, but it is also experienced as an object. She suggests that there are distinctive manners of comportment and move-ment that are associated with women. Young attributes these different modalities, first, to the social spaces in which women learn to comport themselves. In terms of sport this involves constraints of space and repeatedly acting in less assertive and aggressive ways than men. Conversely, from this it might be deduced that men acquire those embodied practices in sport that are aggressive. Rather than women lacking the corporeal capa-cities to perform effectively in sport, through iterative gendered practice they come to throw (run, move, develop sporting practices) 'like a girl'. Second, Young suggests women are encouraged to see themselves through the gaze of others, including the 'male gaze', as developed in the work of Laura

Mulvey (1975), and to become more aware of themselves as objects of the scrutiny of others. The aspirations to the heroic body of the successful athlete might be viewed as informing the dreams and the practices of men in sport. Whereas young women practise the comportment of femininity, young men engage in the techniques of masculinity, embodied in the 'hard man' image of the boxer. Social space is constituted by body practices and culture in which psychic investments are made; the gym is not a world apart. Within gender binaries, not only are women expected to be less physically aggressive, but also their anxieties might assume corporeal expression, for example in contact sports, such as those where aggressive tackling is the norm, such as Australian rules football.

Sport has the capacities to generate ways of being in the world through routine practices and engagements. Sport is both ordinary and spectacular; it is a back and forth dialectic of body practices and of iconography – the raw and the cooked.

Sport is itself cultural and constitutive of culture and is beset by contradictions and ambivalences. Sport may always be raw in a sense because of its enfleshed actualities and the arrangement of people, things and places that make up everyday culture. Sport has endurances and persistences but it is not a linear narrative and even in the everyday there are disruptions and possibilities of change. Sport's great iconic moments and heroic figures and celebrity stars, which inform fandom and identifications, are never entirely absent from the affects that play out in sport's routine practices. These stories are part of the delivery systems that make up sport and intersect with the routine embodied practices and the ways in which bodies are implicated at different sites – in the gym, on the pitch or in informal settings and in sentient spectatorship. This chapter has focused on what might be ordinary and routine; the next highlights another aspect of the mix and considers sport's spectacles and spectacular affects.

7

SPECTACLES, SPECTATORS AND THE SPECTACULAR

Sport offers particular opportunities for display and for spectatorship. This chapter addresses some of the questions raised earlier about sport and belonging and the identifications that the display of sport invokes, and argues that both have been transformed through new technologies. Sporting identifications have powerful inflections because sport has its own intensities and expression through embodied performance and display, and sport creates and sustains the most passionate of personal investments. Sport dominates media pages, images and broadcasting schedules, which create some of the imaginaries in which participants invest. Sensation is multifaceted and diverse in its interpretations. It can involve sensory experience, sometimes sensationalism, as in media representations, and the interrelationship between spectators and performers, in what can be the unmediated relationship between the event and its perception and reception and the effects of spectators on the sporting event and its effects on them. Given the intensity of the experience in many sporting examples, the concept of sensation is part of the two-way process in the liminal space between the movement on the field of play and the responses of those who watch. These are elements in what transforms a game or a sporting event into a spectacle (Bourdieu, 1986).

Spectacles are not only those that are manufactured through the commodification of sport. The discourse of sport is immersed in taxonomies of 'great moments' that often involve great sports stars, more heroes than celebrities; a distinction that increasingly has to be made in modern, commodified sport. For example Mike Marqusee (2005) argues that Muhammad Ali is a sports hero, whereas Michael Jordan is a superstar and celebrity. The politics of race have played a big part in the making of sports' heroes, for example, Jesse Owens, to Hitler's anger, debunked Nazi propaganda of Aryan supremacy by winning four gold medals in Berlin in 1936. Jackie Robinson, the first African American major league baseball player who played for the Brooklyn Dodgers starting in 1947 is also part of this history.

Marqusee's argument about heroes in sport focuses on Ali but also on politics. Ali has engaged in activities that others could and have followed, for example in terms of his political activism, whereas there are very few who could do what Michael Jordan did. According to Marqusee,

> there is ... no way we can emulate Michael Jordan ... In contrast we can all emulate at least some of what Ali did outside the ring ... the adherence to conscience in defiance of social pressure, the expression of self through a commitment to a higher cause and a wider community. It was the willingness of the Greatest [Ali frequently used the cry 'I am the Greatest' prior to fights] to link his destiny to the littlest that won him the devotion of so many.
>
> *(Marquseee, 2005:295–97)*

Nonetheless, when Michael Jordan retired the world press was saturated with hyperbole: 'God wore number 23' (*Di Morgen*,

Germany); 'God is going home' (*Yedioth Ahrnonoth*, Israel); 'God will never fly again' (*Asahi Shimbun*, Japan); 'Tell us it's not true' (*El País*, Spain); 'A myth that has gone beyond sports' (*El Periódico*, Spain) (cited in Miller *et al.*, 2001).

The inclusion of particular athletes, whether heroes or superstars or just incredibly competent (although stardust helps) also creates some of the categories of sports' great moments, not all of which have been spectacular, but each has assumed the elements of the spectacle, which Bourdieu (1986) notes in the transformation of the event into the spectacle. Women are less well represented in these moments and in the line of heroes, but some do achieve heroic status, if not on a par with Ali. Laila Ali, as Ali's daughter and a boxer of some renown, must have a place. As must Dame Kelly Holmes, the double gold medallist in the 500 and 1500 metres. Some of these elements have come together. Rivalries such as that between Steve Ovett and Sebastian Coe in 1980 created feelings of excitement that put their races onto the list. Record breaking counts, such as Roger Bannister's breach of the 4 minute mile in 1954 or more recently Usain Bolt's incredible achievements in the 100 metres, especially in 2008 and 2009, made him the sprinter everyone wanted to watch. (The high expectations of Bolt made his disqualification in the World Championships in 2011 at Daegu, for two false starts, all the more dreadful.) Records matter in the making of these great moments, even more so when they might be less expected, such as Lynn Davies at the Olympics in the long jump in 1968, or even more surprisingly given her extreme lack of experience in the sport, Nancy Lopez winning the amateur golf championship in New Mexico in 1969. A perfect score, such as that of Nadia Comaneci, the Romanian gymnast, at the 1976 Olympics is one of those beautiful but quantifiable moments that goes down as one of sport's moments. A great moment can involve a team rather than individuals: Welsh rugby teams through the 1970s with Gareth Davies, Barry John and J. P. R. Williams; the Llanelli Scarlets who beat the New Zealand All

Blacks at Stradey Park 9–3 in 1972. The team no longer plays at Stradey and is no longer called just the Scarlets, but 'Who beat the All Blacks but good old Sospan Fach' is still sung at games.

More widely England's success in the 1966 men's football World Cup still permeates football chants and the collective consciousness in a manner that could be more entrenched because of the lack of any such success since. Diego Maradona's goal of the century in the quarter final against England in the 1986 World Cup is usually included on lists.

Many big moments do involve individuals; boxing's great spectacles also contribute to this phenomenon: Rocky Marciano's fights, the Rumble in the Jungle in Kinshasa between George Foreman and Muhammad Ali in 1974; the Fight of the Century between Joe Frazier and Muhammad Ali at Madison Square Garden in 1971. It is, however, the fight itself that makes the moment. The people, the boxers, their promoters, trainers, cut men, the umpire, the spectators, the activity, the light, the sound, the movement are all caught up the whirlpool of the event. Intentionality is all part of this mix and it is the ways in which these elements combine that make these spectacles.

Sometimes teams and even victories are condensed into an individual: Botham's Ashes in 1981, when Ian Botham contributed with bat and ball to an amazing reversal of fortune for England against Australia. The top ten depends on who is compiling the list and US versions always include Michael Phelps' stunning achievements in the pool: his six gold medals and two bronzes at Athens in 2004 and his eight gold medals at the 2008 summer Games. Such achievements may place more emphasis on that which is quantified than feeling and passion given the magnitude, but it is a fine line between calculating for the record books and gauging the levels of excitement. Some great moments omit the human agent altogether, which demonstrates the specificities of sport: Red Rum winning the Grand National in 1977 is a case in point.

This is a far from comprehensive list and it will be difficult for readers who are sports fans not to feel aggrieved at the exclusion of what they consider to be a great, if not the greatest, moment in sport. This is what sport does. It is impossible not to be drawn in and to feel the injustice of the referee who makes a decision against your team or to discuss the greatest team ever – even imaginary ones. Our imaginations are informed by the spectacles we have seen, but there are also more specific and more local investments in sport and it is very hard to stand outside. We may mask our feelings with reference to that which can be quantified and measured, but what matters is whose side you are on and your identifications. Sport generates strong feelings.

Not that sport is all about heroes and spectacles, or even celebrity stars, although the media preoccupation with superstars makes it difficult to avoid.

Whilst much of the activity that is classified as sport is routine and everyday in the training schedules of athletes or the everyday or sporadic engagements of amateurs who occasionally participate in an activity, such as a kick-about in the park or go to the gym or go swimming, much of the attraction of sport and certainly what is most visible and voluble about sport is its spectacles and mega events. The mechanisms of representation and symbolic systems, and the phenomenon of media display and the big event are part of the politics of spectacle and spectatorship (Sugden and Tomlinson, 2011; Houlihan, 2008; Miller *et al.*, 2001).

In/visible women

Gender has played a key part in analyses of the coverage of sporting spectacles (Markula, 2009) and is a constituent of the properties sport has for promoting wider participation as well as sustaining enduring aspects of exclusion. Demonstrating the invisibility of women in the public arena of representation has a long history in feminist critiques. Women have been 'hidden from history' to quote the title of Sheila Rowbotham's famous 1974 book, or they have been an 'absent presence', as claimed in the work of French psychoanalytic feminists (Irigaray, 1984, 1991; Cixous, 1980 in Marks and Courtviron, 1980). History, and none more so than the history of sport, has often been written as if only white men from the middle and upper classes were agents and protagonists who matter. We know the stories that feature men because they are recorded, but women, if mentioned at all, are frequently relegated to the domestic sphere of familial and intimate relationships, where they are assumed to be present even though they are absent from what is made visible, for example as mothers, who often do not even need to be named (Irigaray, 1984). Women 'just are'. Motherhood is recognised in the discourses of sport within the context of moral disapproval, for example when women climbers leave their children to engage in the perceived dangerous sport of mountaineering. There is also a long tradition of using women's reproductive capacities as justification of their exclusion from sport. Women have been absent and invisible and yet they are also present because what women do is taken for granted. This raises questions about the capacities of sport to promote diversity and cohesion and, in the case of sex gender, about where women are in the sporting family and in the communities of sport.

The slippery nature of in/visible women in sport presents problems for the researcher. Women are increasingly visible in sport; they belong to an empirical category of persons defined by sex. There are women and men and the gender binary is embedded in the rules of the game. Sex gender, however, emerges as a problem because sometimes classifying sex is problematic, as is evident in the coverage of gender verification testing. Whatever the panoply of gender verification testing apparatuses that are utilised in sport, the outcome of the visibility of such testing is to generate more difficulties and not to establish any certainties.

The female–male dualism may not be as clear as the regulators of sport might hope. Women in the field of sport are certainly not as visible as women increasingly are in other sexualised spaces of the mass media, but they do constitute an empirical, marked category. Men are not usually marked in sport except in athletics. Websites are classified by sport, for example, football, tennis or athletics (the most gender egalitarian of embodied sporting practices) with sub-divisions for women's activities. Women are always a sub-category of the mainstream, male stream web pages. Home pages of sports have links and, although increasingly women are mentioned as a sub-group, sometimes they have to be extracted from classifications such as 'community' or under 'diversity' and 'social inclusion' policies. Anti-racist sites often encompass gender, dis/ability, sexuality and myriad aspects of social exclusion and marginalisation. If women are invisible on the sports web pages, sport may similarly be absent from – or at least not central to – feminist and women's education websites.

Visibility and presence on the stage of the sporting mega event can be a significant factor in promoting inclusion and equal opportunities and the biggest spectacle of the Olympic Games is a mega event that provides more equal coverage than, for example, other mega events such as the Super Bowl or the World Cup.

Sport and the mega event

The role that the media have played, especially in recent years, has been to transmit knowledge about sport through making particular sporting practices and connections visible and audible. Sport always stands for something more than itself; 'always both representing and being represented' (Miller *et al.*, 2001). Sport lends itself to spectacle and sensation; it is more than kicking, hitting or catching a ball, or running or jumping; it is about success and failure, and hopes and aspirations. These may be personal, they may be linked to community, such as a particular team or club, or they may be national, especially as expressed in international competitions. The Olympics are such an international competition, and are a prime example of what have come to be called 'mega events' (Roche, 2000).

Miller *et al.* (2001) suggest that rituals such as the medal ceremonies at the summer Olympic Games epitomise national identification and affect. Such rituals are tableaux of bodily dispositions. The athletes, their bodies draped in the colours and insignia of nation and corporation, are led to the ceremony. Olympic Games' opening ceremonies as rituals are illustrative of sporting mega events where the culture of sport is represented and reproduced, especially through the media coverage that transmits these events across the globe.

In the contemporary world, the label of mega event is increasingly associated with sport or popular entertainment, because of the sponsorship they invite and the profits that can accrue to investors. It is impossible to disentangle the spectacle from the levels of sponsorship, although the relationship is not straightforward or singular in its trajectory.

Sensation, visibility and sound are central to sport and to who is in and who is out, who speaks and how silence is configured. Sensation and affect are implicated in the transformations of events into spectacles and there are connections and disjunctions between spectacles, sensation and what is sensational. Sporting spectacles are contingent and temporally and spatially located in spaces that increasingly include cyberspace and the virtual as well as the actual, as well as being governed by commercial, economic and political factors.

The Olympic Games, especially the opening ceremonies, present a mega spectacle *par excellence*, with Beijing in 2008 being probably the most costly and magnificent to date. Beijing also demonstrated particularly well the assemblage of sounds, sights, light, movement, objects and people caught up in a whirlpool of sensation.

Beijing featured stadiums that have become architectural landmarks. The Beijing National Stadium, the now-famous

Bird's Nest, was full to its 91,000 capacity and provided a stunning display of Chinese culture. The ceremony was directed by Chinese filmmaker Zhang Yimou, who was the chief director. The director of music for the ceremony was composer Chen Qigang. It was noted for its focus on ancient Chinese culture, and for its creativity, as well as being the first to use weather modification technology to prevent rainfall. The final ascent of the torch featured Olympic gymnast Li Ning, who appeared to run through air around the membrane of the stadium. Featuring more than 15,000 performers, including the famous terracotta warriors, the ceremony lasted over four hours and was reported to have cost over $100 million to produce. The opening ceremony was lauded by spectators and various international press as spectacular and spellbinding and by many accounts the greatest ever (Brownell, 2008). The handover of the Olympic flag from the mayor of Beijing to the mayor of London, Boris Johnson, followed by a performance organised by the London Organising Committee of the Olympic and Paralympic Games (LOCOG), which included performances by guitarist Jimmy Page and recording artist Leona Lewis in a closing ceremony, presented something of a contrast between Beijing and London. Whereas Beijing had deployed a vast panoply of visual, aural, sentient techniques whereby to celebrate Chinese cultural inheritance, encompassing art, opera and dance, albeit all prior to the communist era, London relied upon more modest icons of popular contemporary culture, a London bus and David Beckham, who nonetheless embodies a pinnacle of the sports mega star. Celebrity is a crucial component of western cultural practice, increasingly manifest in sport.

The idea of the spectacle is closely enmeshed with visibility and presence, and their counterparts, invisibility and absence. The massive expansion of the media sport nexus means that what passes for sport and the participants in this field are those we see and whose presence is pervasive. This applies to the participants and the sports, and to which sports are represented.

The rituals and spectacles of the Olympic Games are conventionally seen to particularly offer opportunities for the promotion of cultural values as well as products through the visibility of spectacular displays. The presence of the world's media and modern technologies make them especially attractive to sponsors and entrepreneurs as well as governments; this is a global stage on which sports stars perform and goods and values can be promoted through performance, association and display. However, different sites involve different specific practices and different Olympics are generative of different affects that are temporally and spatially situated and configured.

The values that are implicitly and explicitly expressed at these ceremonies, especially the opening ceremonies, are frequently configured around the nation and, in particular, the nation state, which has a powerful position in the assemblages of the modern Olympics: the games offer a stage for the performance of nation which is often denied in other political arenas. The culture of the Games as expressed at the ceremonies is also framed by the Olympic Movement and its ideals, although these are ideals that have largely been betrayed, especially in terms of the celebration of peace and a peace movement for young people (Lenskyj, 2000, 2008; Sugden and Tomlinson, 2011).

The ceremonies demonstrate that sport is to be taken seriously; sport matters. Whatever the hyperbole and the razzmatazz of these mega events, what is at stake is more than 'just entertainment'. Not only are the Games big business, they are also seriously political and offer a site for the enactment of political conflicts, which demand the generation of sensations of emotion and sentient as well as material affects. Sport is also crucial to representation and assemblage of culture and is constitutive of culture through the modes of commerce, politics and nation. The virtual and the representational are inseparable from the enfleshed practices and material dimensions and forces of the Games. Materialities such as financial and economic flows and sponsorship are shaped by as well as shaping the virtual processes of sponsorship.

The Games largely present a very particular version of the nation and the nation state, as bounded and contained, rather than a more open transnational, globalised source of identity. The rituals and symbols deployed at the ceremonies reinforce, reinstate, remember and create traditional national identities that are strongly evocative of the militaristic disciplined body practices of masculinity by which they are performed. This is clearly a place for national patriotic identifications and for political as well as sporting contests, but, although sport is so transparently based on the binary logic of sex, the opening and closing ceremonies are far from transparent in their enactment of masculinity and hegemonic masculinity as performance elides with athletic, enfleshed achievement and, in the big ceremonies, militaristic nationalism.

The Games are global through the range of nations participating and, even more importantly, through the involvement of global corporations and the world media. The opening ceremonies of the Olympics demonstrate the impact of globalisation in all its manifestations and the links between sport, politics, economy and culture, and the inequalities of the contemporary globalised world.

The culture of sport is closely connected to global politics and economics, which is particularly apparent in the sport, media and commerce nexus that plays out in the opening ceremonies of the Olympics to demonstrate the inextricable interconnections between the media and sponsorship, and some of the contradictions as well as synergies between the mega event and the Olympic ideal. Performance of the big events of the Games are as competitive as the enfleshed athletic activities, with each host city and nation attempting to present a spectacle that surpasses all others; Beijing in 2008 being a good example in both the politics and the display of the events and the synthesis of the virtual with the material. The massive displays in which individual people were subsumed into collective waves of light, movement and colour provided a demonstration of the massive scale of population and change in China.

The modern Olympics offer an accumulation of new technologies through which cultural changes take place, all of which is closely enmeshed with the creation and performance of the spectacle and the experience and relationship of spectatorship. This is not a linear narrative of change and progress, although there have been pivotal moments of drama and disruption in the Games. There are remarkable endurances in the disciplined marching of the national groups of athletes, the iteration of the Olympic ideals from the IOC, the magnitude of the stadiums with tiny figures in blocks of nation and similar but more mobile collections of the artists and performers. Spectacles are orchestrated and designed but they also generate and are productive of new relationships and configurations that have political, economic, social and cultural affects as well as reacting to and being formed by them. Spectators and the performance of the event are all caught up in the processes of being, doing, remembering and becoming, where the rituals of the Olympics are experienced in the enfleshed presence of 'being there' or viewed at a distance on television.

Some of the processes of cultural production are manifested in the organisation and management of the opening ceremonies in which media play an important role, not only in the transmission of sporting spectacles but also in their creation. The use of symbols, images and signifiers of nation and athleticism, the choice of music and visual images are all affects of and are affected by current popular cultural forms as portrayed in the entertainment industry, as well as the narratives of national pride and athletic achievement that make up the memories as well as the imaginings of the Olympics. Cultures are reproduced and formed through a mix of technologies, symbols, representations, memories and stories that come together in sporting mega events and spectacles to which visibility and sensation are central.

8

DO WE LIVE ON PLANET SPORT?

There is a massive diversity and range of sports and activities that can be included under the umbrella category of sport. The extent of participation, whether as spectators, followers, practitioners or involvement in the network of commerce and media, that embraces sport and its synergies supports the claim that we live on planet sport. This is not just a matter of size and scale, for example as is illustrated by the global reach of sport and its networks. Sport also engages with the routine and the everyday and with the inner worlds and its connections are not confined to the specificities of its practices. Sport intersects with and informs other areas of experience and generates its own affects in a whole range of fields, ranging from the practical applications of sports science and understandings of embodied practices to the intellectual contributions of the theoretical frameworks that have been developed in exploring the intersections of power axes in what makes up sport and the synergies between sport and other social worlds and fields of inquiry. Sport is both distinctive and powerfully imbricated with other social, political, cultural and economic forces.

Sport is often classified under the heading of culture within governance structures and there are clearly points of connection. Sport, however, has suffered from the binary logic of high and low culture, partly because of its associations with play, which become trivialised within cultural hierarchies, as well, of course, because of the devaluing of enfleshed activities and of the body in another dichotomy, based on the nature-culture, mind-body split. Not only are these distorted dichotomies but they offer inappropriate categorisations of culture and practice. As this book has demonstrated, sport is a rich field of inquiry for the exploration of social relations and social divisions and cultural practices.

The field of sport offers a particularly good example of the relationship between perception and the objects of perception. The material, enfleshed practices of sport are constructed in our heads as well as generating emotive and material affects. The creation of the intensity of feelings that accompanies some aspects of sport, notably spectatorship and the identifications that are made in sport are all part of the mix of events in which we are swept up.

Sport manifests a deceptive binary simplicity that is based on the logic of winning or losing, success or failure, through an embodied set of practices that have little to do with the complexities and subtleties of intellectual creative engagement, a view that is hotly contested by aficionados of many sports, such as cricket. It is, however, not only the complexity of some of the embodied practices of sport on the field that challenges over simplification, but also the synergies between sport and other social worlds and their points of connection. Sport is in many ways distinctive in its diversities, but it is also both reflective of social and cultural changes and continuities, and generative of those social flows and forces. It does seem simple, but not only do systems of politics, culture and economics intersect in the power operations in play in sport, feelings, emotions as well as the commonalities of flesh and material affects are part of the process.

Politics are played out in particular ways in sport, but the take on politics in this book emphasises the possibilities of politics with a small 'p' and has been argued within the framework of the personal as political, as well as acknowledging some of the big moments in sport that have been implicated in global politics. *Planet Sport* demonstrates possibilities for change, but also the strong persistence of inequalities and binaries, which show that, although sport is global and crosses boundaries of nation and sometimes ethnicities and cultures, the nature of sport means that it is still an unequal playing field. This makes sport political, as does the protest that is expressed by organised groups at big sporting events such as the Olympics. Sports constitute events, whether as mega spectacles transmitted to millions by satellite across the globe or as more routine encounters in amateur leagues, friendly games and at the gym. Each is an event in that it brings together different dimensions of social, cultural, economic and political life that intersect with the personal investments of those who are caught up in its excitements and engagements. Sport definitely has distinctive capacities for the creation and inspiration of passionate commitment, strong identifications and enormous pleasure for individuals and collectivities.

As this book has demonstrated, there are parallel discourses of sport that intersect at different points. One dominant discourse embraces sport and policy and emphasises the advantages of sport to the health of the polis, both corporeally and politically. In the sports literature, bodies are often classified within the remit of physiognomy within a dichotomy of nature that embraces biology and culture. Bodies, flesh, muscle and bones belong in the realm of medical science, with the mind and motivation the prerogative of psychology. Just as sex and gender are inextricably interwoven and interconnected so is flesh enmeshed with sporting practice and sports culture. Flesh is what is common to athletes and to spectators, although with less immediacy. Flesh is both commonality and differentiation. It is the shared, rule-governed activities with the pleasures and pains of the flesh that make up the experience of sport and also differentiate between its participants, and flesh and bodies that influence and shape competition and competitive outcomes. The risks and dangers of sport are powerfully enfleshed.

The idea of sport as a healthy set of practices, which create fit bodies and promote team spirit and cooperation and make good citizens, has a powerful presence in the literature of contemporary sport. Another dominant discourse, although one that carries less weight in the apparatuses of governance is that which is evident in the art and literature that sport generates and relates to the passions that sport invokes. Sport offers a particular psychosocial domain in which popular cultural forms and financial incentives collide and sometimes connect with personal desires and aspirations and powerful collective psychic investments. What is distinctive about the set of practices, enfleshed actualities, affects, intensities, expressions and materialities that make up sport is that these regimes intersect in particular ways and provide significant points of connection between diverse fields and have important and meaningful political impacts. Sport is more than knowing the score.

GLOSSARY

AIBA (Association Internationale de Boxe Amateur) organises amateur boxing. AIBA was originally FIBA (Fédération Internationale de Boxe Amateur). The official foundation of FIBA was in 1920 at the Games in Antwerp. It was beset by scandals in the Second World War and reformed in 1946, when the English Amateur Boxing Association, in partnership with the French Boxing Federation, created AIBA. Currently AIBA continues to govern Olympic Games boxing. The word 'amateur' is no longer used, and the organisation seeks to influence and regulate boxing throughout the world with a commitment to the elimination of corrupt practices, especially drug abuse.

Australian rules football began in Melbourne in 1858 and is the most popular sport in Australia, especially in terms of spectatorship; football has the highest attendance of all sports in Australia. There are two teams of eleven players with points scored through goals; handling of the ball is permitted and of the twenty-two players, eighteen are on the field, with four interchange players. The ball and the pitch are elliptical and there are not the set positions of either soccer or rugby. Most significantly it is not only a very fast-moving contact sport but one marked by a great deal of physical contact and a large number of whole body tackles. The sport and its embodied practices are deeply embedded in sporting masculinities. Women play with a smaller ball than men and have modified tackling rules and have come into the game much more recently – fifty years after the men's game started.

EWBL (Exclusively Women's Basketball League) provides a platform for women, particularly from Muslim and other ethnic-minority communities in the UK to gain competitive experience as players, coaches, officials and spectators in an environment that its website notes is sensitive to their religious and cultural needs. The organisation is linked to the MWSF (see www.mwsf.org.uk/ewbl.html).

FA (Football Association) was founded in 1863 as the governing body of the game in England. The FA is responsible for all regulatory aspects of the game of football in England including the women's game, on which its record is not good (see WFA). Its stated aims include promoting the development of the game amongst all ages, backgrounds and abilities in terms of participation and quality to the greatest possible number of people. The FA regulates the game on and off the field of play through the 'Laws of the Game' and the 'Rules of The Association' and sanctioning, either directly or indirectly, all matches, leagues and competitions played in England. It oversees the administration of the disciplinary system and the administration of refereeing throughout the game. The FA organises senior men's, youth and women's national competitions and England national representative teams in international matches, most notably the men's senior team in the FIFA World Championships and the UEFA European Championships and friendly fixtures.

FIFA (Fédération Internationale de Football Association) was founded in Paris in 1904 by the representatives of the associations in France, Belgium, Denmark, Netherlands, Spain, Sweden and Switzerland. Since 2007 FIFA has included 208 member associations, thus making it one of the biggest sports federations in the world. The scope of popularity of the sport of football is recognised by FIFA in its promotional websites. The president, the eighth in FIFA's history since 1998, has been Sepp Blatter, who was elected as successor to Dr João Havelange. FIFA also regulates the women's game. It remains a male-dominated organisation, although it now has stated commitments to promote the women's game and improve women's competitions.

IAAF (International Amateur Athletic Federation) was founded in 1912 by 17 national athletic federations to establish a governing authority for an athletic programme, for standardised technical equipment and world records. In 1982, the IAAF abandoned the traditional concept of amateurism and in 1985 created trust funds for athletes. The IAAF currently has 212 national federations. The IAAF has been heavily involved worldwide in the development and application of an extensive anti-doping programme involving testing both in and out of competition.

ICC (International Cricket Council) is the international governing body of cricket based, somewhat surprisingly, in Dubai, that organises competitions, promotes the game and sets standards and is the decision-making body for the women's as well as the men's sport. As with most governing bodies in sport, the women's game is a sub-section (in the case of the ICC, under Match Zone) of the organisation.

IOC (International Olympic Committee) is the international governing body of the modern Olympic Games established in Lausanne in Switzerland in 1894 prior to the first games of the modern era, which were held in Athens in 1896, and subsequently the winter games, the first of which were in France in 1924. The IOC serves to support and promote the Olympic Movement, the principles of which are expressed in the Charter that has been extensively amended to promote more egalitarian democratic principles through the history of the modern games (including wider participation by women). Membership remains largely male but there is evidence of incremental change (see www.olympic.org/content/the-ioc/the-ioc-institution1/ioc-members-list/). The Women and Sport Commission now advises the IOC on the promotion of women in sport if not on its regulatory bodies. The IOC began as a body dominated by white, largely aristocratic men but has responded to change and to accusations of bribery and corruption, especially following the Salt Lake City scandal that erupted in 1998 over the hosting of the games. There has been a proliferation of other committees that work with the IOC: NOCs (National Organising Committees), OCOGs (local Organising Committees in the host city) and IFs (International sports Federations).

IFBA (International Female Boxing Association) was formed in 1997 to regulate and promote women's boxing. One of its founding aims was to persuade the IOC to include women's boxing in the Olympics, in which it was successful for 2012. IFBA sets standards and rules for the women's sport.

IPC (International Paralympic Committee) was founded in 1989. It is the global governing body of the Paralympic Movement, made up of elected representatives, and includes 170 National Paralympic Committees and organises the summer and winter Paralympic Games, and serves as the International Federation for nine sports, for which it supervises and coordinates the World Championships and other competitions as an umbrella organisation representing several sports and disabilities. The IPC is keen to stress the growth of the Paralympics. More countries competed at the Beijing 2008 Paralympics (3,951 athletes, 146 countries) than in the Munich 1972 Olympic Games. In Beijing, the degree of media coverage was unprecedented. The task of the IPC is becoming more challenging as debates about what constitutes disability and the difficulties of differentiating between aids to disabled athletes and performance enhancement become more complex.

IPL (Indian Premier League) was set up to organise and control the short (twenty over) competitions of Twenty 20 cricket in India. It was initiated by the BCCI (Board of Control for Cricket in India) and has been enormously successful in providing entertaining cricket with massive investment and high rewards for players. In 2010 it was broadcast live on YouTube, reflecting its popularity and its populism. It breaks with the conservative traditions of test and county cricket as well as the subtleties of test matches. Its new approach to the traditional long slow game is not universally popular and not everyone has been drawn by the razzmatazz and pace of the games but players are attracted by the money and it is a lucrative development that is keeping the game alive, whilst transforming some of its embodied practices in the field. IPL has done little for the women's game and women are often included as part of the sexualised entertainment prior to the men's Twenty 20 competitions. The games are fast moving and very entertaining, however.

ITF (International Tennis Federation) was set up in 1911 in Paris as a world governing body for tennis. By that time lawn tennis was beginning to develop rapidly worldwide and it seemed natural that National Associations that were already established should come together to form a liaison whereby the universal game would be uniformly structured.

MLB (Major League Baseball), founded in the nineteenth century, is the highest level of professional baseball in the US and Canada, comprising teams that play in the National League and American League. Thirty teams participate, each one a men's team.

MWSF (Muslim Women's Sports Foundation) aims to provide opportunities for women from black and minority ethnic communities to participate in a variety of sports without compromising their religious or cultural values. Through catering to and raising awareness of their needs they aim to increase the numbers of black and minority ethnic women involved in sport through different activities, such as playing, coaching, refereeing and volunteering (see www.mwsf.org. uk/the_mwsf.html).

NBA (National Basketball Association) is the preeminent men's professional basketball league in North America, with thirty franchised clubs founded in 1946. The sport has increased enormously in popularity, not least because of its superstars, notably Michael Jordan who played for the Chicago Bulls. The Women's National Basketball Association (**WNBA**) is the women's professional basketball league, founded in 1996, which in spite of the links between netball and basketball is not quite as popular as the men's game. It has twelve teams.

PGA (Professional Golf Association) organises the relevant PGA tours; there is one in Europe and one in North America.

R & A (Royal and Ancient) assumes responsibility for the administration of the Rules of Golf with the consent of 143 organisations from the amateur and professional game, and on behalf of over 30 million golfers in 126 countries throughout Europe, Africa, Asia-Pacific and the Americas. It is based at St Andrews but is not actually part of the golf club.

WFA (Women's Football Association) was formed in 1969. In spite of the popularity of the women's game (in 1920 53,000 watched Dick Kerr's Ladies beat St Helen's, 4–0) the FA banned women from playing on Football League grounds in 1921 because the game was deemed unsuitable for females and ought not to be encouraged. Since 1983 the WFA has been affiliated to the FA on the same basis as County Football Associations. The Women's Super League, an eight-team competition was started in 2011 to promote the women's game.

WBA (World Boxing Association) was born as the National Boxing Association (NBA) in 1921, in Rhode Island, as an entity devoted to the government and control of this professional activity, with limited jurisdiction in the US. The NBA set up world-recognised heavyweight championships, such as Dempsey vs. Filippo, Dempsey vs. Carpetier and Big Hands 'The Killer' vs. Tunney. The WBA has attempted to centralise the universal promotion of boxing.

WBAN (Women's Boxing Archive Network) is a subscription-based US web resource for news and information on women's boxing competitions and women's boxing as well as providing histories of the women's sport and detailed information about boxers past and present. Much of the general information can be accessed free but additional material is only available to subscribers.

REFERENCES

Baseball Milwaukee (2011) 'Story of baseball', www.storyofbaseball. com/about-baseball.php (last accessed, 12 December 2011)

BBC (2011) 'Too fast to be a woman', 14 May, www.bbc.co.uk/ programmes/b00yrv05 (last accessed, 20 May 2011)

Bourdieu, B. (1986) *Distinction: A Social Critique of the Judgement of Taste*, trans. R. Nice, London: Routledge.

Braidotti, R. (1994) *Nomadic Subjects: Embodiment and Sexual Difference in Contemporary Feminist Theory*, New York: Columbia University Press.

Briggs, A. (1995) *A History of Broadcasting in the United Kingdom*, vols I–V, Oxford: Oxford University Press.

Brownell, S. (2008) *Beijing's Olympics: What the Olympics Mean to China*, New York: Rowman and Littlefield.

Butler, J. (1990) *Gender Trouble: Feminism and the Subversion of Identity*, London: Routledge.

Butler, J. (1993) *Bodies That Matter: On the Discursive Limits of Sex*, London: Routledge.

Cixous, H. (1980) 'Sorties' in *La Femme Née*, Paris: Union Générale d'Éditions.

Connell, R. W. (1995) *Masculinities*, Cambridge: Cambridge University Press.

Coover, R. (1971) *The Universal Baseball Association, inc J. Henry Waugh Prop*, New York: Plume.

Csikzentimihalyi, M. (1975) *Beyond Boredom and Anxiety: Experiencing Flow in Work and Play*, San Francisco: Jossey Bass.

De Beauvoir, S. (1989 [1949]) *The Second Sex*, trans. H. Parsley, New York: Vintage Books.

Egan, P. (2006 [1812]) *Boxiana, Sketches of Ancient and Modern Pugilism from the Days of the Renowned Broughton and Slack to the Championship of Cribb*, vol. 1, London: Elibron Classics Adamant Media.

Foucault, M. (1981) *The History of Sexuality, Volume 1. An Introduction*, trans. R. Hurley, Harmondsworth: Penguin.

Giulianotti, R (2005) *Sport: A Critical Sociology*, Cambridge: Polity.

Gold, J. R. and Gold, M. M. (eds) (2008) *Olympic Cities: City Agendas, Planning and the World's Games, 1896–2012*, London: Routledge.

Goldblatt, D. (2007) *The Ball is Round*, London: Penguin Viking.

Guttmann, A. (2005) *Sport the First Five Millennia*, Amherst, Boston, MA: University of Massachusetts Press.

Hadfield, T. (2010) *Barnsley FC: My Club My Passion*, Walsall: SR Print Management.

Haraway, D. (2003) *The Companion Species Manifesto: Dogs, People and Significant Others*, Chicago: Prickly Paradigm Press.

Hargreaves, J. (1994) *Sporting Females: Critical Issues in the History and Sociology of Women's Sport*, London: Routledge.

Hargreaves, J. (2000) *Heroines of Sport: The Politics of Difference and Identity*, London: Routledge.

Hargreaves, J., Vertinsky, P. and McDonald, I. (eds) (2007) *Physical Culture, Power and the Body*, London: Taylor and Francis.

Hauser, T. (1991) *Muhammad Ali. His Life and Times*, New York: Simon and Schuster.

Hornby, N. (2010) *Fever Pitch*, Harmondsworth: Penguin.

Horne, J. (2006) *Sport in Consumer Culture*, Basingstoke: Palgrave.

Houlihan, B. (ed.) (2008) *Sport and Society*, 2nd edition, London: Sage.

Ingham, A. G. and Loy, J. W. (eds) (1993) *Sport in Social Development: Traditions, Transitions, and Transformations*, Champaign, Illinois: Human Kinetics.

Irigaray, L. (1984) *Speculum of the Other Woman*, trans. G. Gill, Ithaca, New York: Cornell University Press.

Irigaray, L. (1991) 'This sex which is not one' in Whitford, M. (ed.) *The Irigaray Reader*, Oxford: Basil Blackwell.

James, C. L. R. (1963) *Beyond a Boundary*, London: Stanley Paul Hutchinson.

James, C. L. R. (2007 [1963]) 'The proof of the pudding' in Tomlinson, A. (ed.) *The Sports Studies Reader*, London: Routledge.

KIO (Kick it Out) (2011) 'Home page about us', www.kickitout.org/ (last accessed 12 December 2011)

Kuper, S. (2003) *Football Against the Enemy*, Littlehampton: Orion.

Lafferty, Y. and McKay, J. (2004) '"Suffragettes in satin shorts?" Gender and competitive boxing', *Qualitative Sociology*, 27 (3): 249–76.

Lemert, C., Elliott, A., Chaffee, D. and Hsu, E. (2010) *Globalization: A Reader*, London: Routledge.

Lenskyj, H. J. (2007) *Inside the Olympic: Power, Politics and Activism*, New York: State University of New York Press.

Lenskyj, H. J. (2008) *Olympic Industry Resistance: Challenging Olympic Power and Propaganda*, SUNY Series on Sport, Culture and Social Relations, Albany: State University of New York Press.

Loy, J. W. (1968) 'The nature of sport: A definitional effort', *Quest*, 10: 1–15.

Marks, E. and Courtviron, I. (eds) (1980) *New French Feminisms: An Anthology*, Amherst, MA: University of Massachusetts Press.

Markula, P. (2009) *Olympic Women and the Media: International Perspectives*, London: Palgrave.

Marqusee, M. (2005) *Redemption Song: Muhammad Ali and the Spirit of the Sixties*, London: Verso.

Merleau-Ponty, M. (1962) *Phenomenology of Perception*, New York: Routledge.

McPherson, B. D., Curtis, J. E. and Loy, J. W. (1989) *The Social Significance of Sport: An Introduction to the Sociology of Sport*, Champaign, Illinois: Human Kinetics.

Miller, T., Lawrence, G., MacKay, J. and Rowe, D. (2001) *Globalization and Sport*, London: Sage.

Moi, T. (1999) *What is a Woman and Other Essays*, Oxford: Oxford University Press.

Mulvey, L. (1975) 'Visual pleasure and narrative cinema', *Screen*, 16 (3): 6–18.

Nandy, A. (1989) *The Tao of Cricket: On Games of Destiny and the Destiny of Games*, New Delhi: Oxford University Press.

Oates, J. C. (1987) *On Boxing*, London: Harper Collins.

O'Connor, D. (2002) (ed.) *Iron Mike: A Mike Tyson Reader*, New York: Thunder's Mouth Press.

Patmore, C. (2012 [1867]) *The Angel in the House*, available at www.victorianweb.org/authors/patmore/angel/ (last accessed, 26 February 2012).

Preuss, H. (2006) *The Economics of Staging the Olympics*, Cheltenham: Edward Elgar.

Rinehart, R. and Sydnor, S. (eds) (2003) *To the Extreme: Alternative Sports, Inside and Out*, Albany: State University of New York Press.

Rinehart, R. and Sydnor, S. (2010) 'Alternative sport and affect: Non representational theory examined', *Sport in Society*, 13 (7): 1268–91.

Roche, M. (2000) *Mega-events and Modernity: Olympics and Expos in the Growth of Global Culture*, London: Routledge.

Rose, N. (1996) *Inventing Ourselves*, Cambridge: Cambridge University Press.

Rowbotham, S. (1974) *Hidden from History: 300 Years of Women's Oppression and the Fight Against It*, London: Pluto Press.

Royal and Ancient (2011) 'Rules and amateur status', www.randa.org/en/Rules-and-Amateur-Status/Etiquette.aspx (last accessed, 26 February 2012)

Scannell, P. and Cardiff, D. (1991) *A Social History of British Broadcasting*, London: Basil Blackwell.

Shilling, C. (2008) *The Body and Social Theory*, 3rd edition, London: Sage.

Sillitoe, A. (2007) *The Loneliness of the Long Distance Runner*, London: Harper Perennial.

Simmons, J. (1988) *Beyond the Ring: The Role of Boxing in American Society*, Chicago: University of Illinois Press.

Stewart, K. (2007) *Ordinary Affects,* Durham, NC: Duke University Press.

Sugden, J. and Tomlinson, A. (2011) *Watching the Olympics: Politics, Power and Representation*, London: Routledge.

Tönnies, F. (1957) *Community and Society. Gemeinschaft and Gesellschaft*, trans. Charles P. Loomis, Michigan: Mighigan State University Press.

WacQuant, L. (2001) 'Whores, slaves and stallions: Languages of exploitation and accommodation among professional fighters', *Body and Society*, 7: 181–94.

WacQuant, L. (2004) *Body and Soul: Notebooks of an Apprentice Boxer*, Oxford: Oxford University Press.

Weber, M. (2003 [1905]) *The Protestant Ethic and the Spirit of Capitalism*, New York: Courier Dover Publications.

Whiting, R. (1971) *Tokyo Underworld*, London: Random House.

Wollstonecraft, M. (2001[1792]) *Vindication of the Rights of Woman*, www.bartleby.com/144/5.html (last accessed, 25 February 2012).

Woodward, K. (2006) *Boxing Masculinity and Identity: The 'I' of the Tiger*, London: Routledge.

Woodward, K. (2009) *Embodied Sporting Practices: Regulating and Regulatory Bodies*, Basingstoke: Palgrave MacMillan.

Woodward, K. (2011) 'The culture of boxing: Sensation and affect', *Sport and History*, 31 (4): 487–503.

Woodward, K. (2012) Sex, Power and the Games, Basingstoke: Palgrave (forthcoming).

Woodward, K., Goldblatt, D. and Wyllie, J. (2011) 'British fair play: Sport across diasporas at the BBC World Service' in McGlynn, C., Mycock, A. and McAuley, J. W. (eds) *Britishness, Identity and Citizenship: The View from Abroad*, Bern, Peter Lang.

Young, I. M. (2005) 'Throwing like a girl' in Young, I. M. (ed.) *On Female Body Experience*, Oxford: Oxford University Press.

INDEX

Taylor & Francis

eBooks

FOR LIBRARIES

ORDER YOUR
FREE 30 DAY
INSTITUTIONAL
TRIAL TODAY!

Over 22,000 eBook titles in the Humanities,
Social Sciences, STM and Law from some of the
world's leading imprints.

Choose from a range of subject packages or create your own!

Benefits for **you**

▶ Free MARC records
▶ COUNTER-compliant usage statistics
▶ Flexible purchase and pricing options

Benefits for your **user**

▶ Off-site, anytime access via Athens or referring URL
▶ Print or copy pages or chapters
▶ Full content search
▶ Bookmark, highlight and annotate text
▶ Access to thousands of pages of quality research
  at the click of a button

For more information, pricing enquiries or to order
a free trial, contact your local online sales team.

UK and Rest of World: **online.sales@tandf.co.uk**

US, Canada and Latin America:
e-reference@taylorandfrancis.com

www.ebooksubscriptions.com

ALPSP Award for
BEST eBOOK
PUBLISHER
2009 Finalist

Taylor & Francis eBooks
Taylor & Francis Group

A flexible and dynamic resource for teaching, learning and research.